S*i*X.
LITTLE HEADS

The 1905 Amesbury Murders

NEIL BERRETT

© Neil Berrett, 2024

Published by Neil Berrett

A Time Unraveller Project

Contact sixlittleheads@timeunraveller.com

A CIP catalogue record for this book is available from the British Library.

ISBN 978-1-0685009-0-9

Typeset by Clare Brayshaw

Cover design by Molly Shah and Clare Brayshaw.
Drawings by Molly Shah

Prepared and printed by:

York Publishing Services Ltd
64 Hallfield Road
Layerthorpe
York YO31 7ZQ

Tel: 01904 431213

Website: www.yps-publishing.co.uk

To Ann and our five, who all fledged and flew.

And for Monkey, Joan, Amy, Florence,
and the six little souls.

*"Somebody might have come along that way
who would have asked him his trouble. But
nobody did come, because nobody does; and
under the crushing recognition of his gigantic
error, Jude continued to wish himself out of
the world."*

Jude The Obscure
Thomas Hardy, 1895

Contents

Head Family Tree

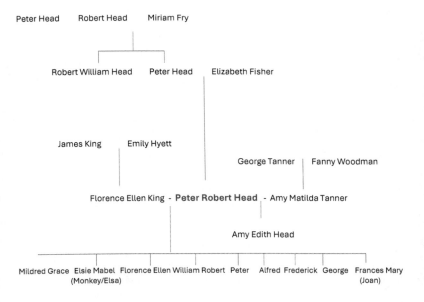

Peter Head   Robert Head   Miriam Fry

Robert William Head   Peter Head   Elizabeth Fisher

James King   Emily Hyett

George Tanner | Fanny Woodman

Florence Ellen King - **Peter Robert Head** - Amy Matilda Tanner

Amy Edith Head

Mildred Grace   Elsie Mabel   Florence Ellen   William   Robert   Peter   Alfred   Frederick   George   Frances Mary
(Monkey/Elsa)   (Joan)

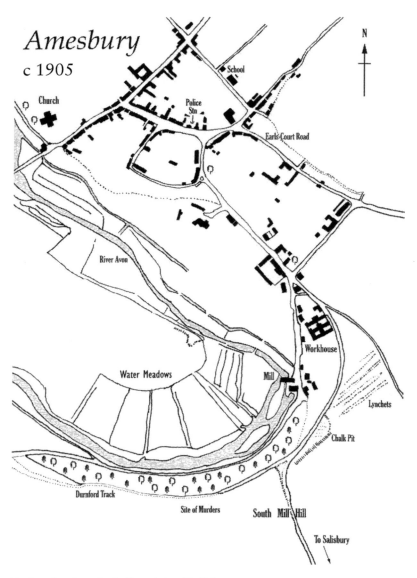

Amesbury

c 1905

N

Church

School

Police
Stn

Earls Court Road

River Avon

Workhouse

Water Meadows

Mill

Lynchets

Chalk Pit

Durnford Track

Site of Murders

South Mill Hill

To Salisbury

Map drawn by and reproduced with permission of Jim Fuller

Introduction

This is no whodunnit.

Peter Robert Head brutally murdered six of his children aged between three months and ten years old. He saw no future and made the decision that they were better off not having one at all, took them into a field and sliced open their throats. He lined up the bodies of his three older sons, while his two daughters and baby son were left where they fell. Then he turned the blade on himself.

That is what happened. He made a grieving widow of his wife and left her to cope alone with such an unimaginable loss. He left a 17-year-old daughter from his first marriage, who had always idolised her father, traumatised and bewildered. He left another daughter, because he did not find her on that fateful day, to live a life with the weight of that incident bearing upon her shoulders as the only survivor among her full siblings. He left an unborn child destined to enter a world of unspoken rumours; the youngest of nine, but only aware of one full sister.

Peter Head left three letters expressing his intention and despair, but they brought no real answers. So, who was Peter Head and what kind of life does a person lead before coming to such a decision?

As a nation, we come together in revulsion at the murder of a child. The Moors Murderers, Brady and Hindley, were universally vilified for the rest of their incarcerated lives. The case of nurse Lucy Letby, convicted of murdering babies in her care has horrified the country far more recently. Serial killers, similarly, are at first feared, then despised; but serial killers of children are a different category of criminal altogether. Hated by other criminals, and considered inhuman.

There is, however, something different about Peter Robert Head. His name did not go into social history as a renowned child murderer. His name is not even in the collective consciousness of the small community in Amesbury, Wiltshire, where the crimes were committed. There is some awareness of the fact that the town's history includes a terrible murder of children, but there is no malevolence around the name of Peter Head. He is no Jack the Ripper, yet he killed more than Jack is 'credited' with. If serial killing is about numbers, Peter Robert Head is a serial killer, too. He murdered six children in the coldest manner one could think of. Had these been random, unrelated children, he would be the demonic child killer of Amesbury; but they were his children, and he is not. Their names have been forgotten, yet we remember many names of children murdered by strangers. It is almost as if society accepts the murder of the murderer's children just a fraction more. Were Peter Head's actions a malignant manifestation of his love, and, if so, what difference, if any, does that make to the legacy of his actions? Actions that indeed did reverberate down the generations, quietly and at times covertly.

After the murders, the event was rarely referred to again publicly. It was never mentioned in the community magazine. The school logbook contained no record beyond the day by the crime, and though it was spoken of down the generations by the townspeople of Amesbury, nobody knew what happened to the family after the event.

Most cannot begin to imagine the trauma, heartbreak and suffering endured by a mother of so many murdered children and how she could ever move forward and cope with that magnitude of loss. What would you expect from a mother who lost six children in such horrific circumstances? For instance, how protective might she be towards her one surviving child? Perhaps you might expect that she would hold on for dear life, never allowing the remaining child out of her sight. To be the guardian she hadn't been to the others. The mother in this story sent her surviving child to an orphanage only months after the murders. The child had lost her six siblings and her beloved father and was then uprooted and sent away from her mother and from everything and everyone that she had known.

I served as a police officer in Wiltshire Police for over thirty years and was a detective for twenty of those. I was involved in the investigation of several Wiltshire murders, conducted Coroner's enquiries for several suicides, and was trained as, and became experienced as, a hostage and crisis intervention negotiator, enabling me thankfully to prevent, or in some cases delay, a number of suicides. I learned that given the chance to talk it through, people in deep mental anguish or crisis could often see through the fog. I have also seen the results of those who didn't give themselves that chance.

Peter Head was clear to his wife on his low opinion of people who took their own lives, as we will see.

There were conflicting views as to how Head seemed in the days before the murders and the question of whether it was preventable is really rhetorical. Those in authority cannot read minds, and those who perpetrate such awful crimes are solely responsible for their actions. Researching Head's life before the murders, I found an interesting and conflicted character.

During my police service, I had not been aware of this largest mass murder in the county's history. I came across the Amesbury murders by chance while researching a friend's family tree: a descendant of Francis Everett, who was a butcher in Amesbury in the early 1900s. His daughter, Mary Harriett, died in August 1905 and appeared in the burial register just before Peter Head. I was drawn by the record of several burials with the same surname buried on the same day. Francis would have met and known the Head family. Coincidentally, Francis Everett would also sit as a juror at the inquest for the dead children.

This is the story of those murders, and, more importantly, it is about the people who were there before, during and afterwards. People who were present in the prelude to the event and those not born at the time, but whose lives were affected by it. It is about the surviving victims forging their way in the world that had been so cruel. Real people who lived, loved, and laughed as we do. People who felt pain and sorrow, joy and happiness, and everything in between.

It is about a standard rural family navigating the hardships of life at the turn of the twentieth century. It is about survival and resilience, luck, and misfortune.

I have chosen not to fill the book with notations and references as to where I found the information. This came from a number of sources: British civil or parish records and census returns, extensive searching of contemporary British newspapers, and also from descendants of the family who were kind enough to indulge me by answering endless questions and who I will mention in the acknowledgements at the end.

All the information I record here is fact, and where I have made slight assumptions or have assessed the meaning of certain facts, it is obvious that I have done so.

Neil Berrett
Wiltshire, 2024

CHAPTER 1

Madame Mathiot, The Monkey

In the early 1980s, Peter Cotterell posed for a photograph with his aunt, Madame Elsa Mathiot, outside the Palace of Versailles. Madame Mathiot was very fond of her nephew. At this point in her life she did not speak to his mother, her younger sister, but Peter she loved, even though he was named after the person who had killed her other siblings.

Madame Mathiot was, by then, becoming frail, forgetful, and slightly more eccentric. Into her late 80s, she carried her belongings in a plastic carrier bag as she kept losing her handbag, and the wig she wore to cover her own thinning hair was, itself, going bald. They had visited the Palace together before. The drive was a good hour from her home in Vernon, in the Northern French region of Eure, situated by the banks of the Seine. Elsa Mathiot enjoyed it there. It was close to the Paris that she had lived in for so many years of her young adulthood and she felt more at home in France than her native England. But being English, she had been an outsider. Elsa had always been an outsider; a step away from the party.

Peter and his wife, Barbara, returned Elsa to the hotel where she had lived for some years. Being estranged from her husband at the time of his death, she had inherited nothing, and his house had gone to his sister.

Elsa lived from day to day in the hotel in Vernon. The lack of a restaurant and the strict rule of being out of the hotel between the hours of 10am and 4pm compelled her, regardless of the weather, to venture out every day into the town to eat or visit the few friends who were still alive. On occasion, she would be seen in the village of Saint-Pierre-d'Autils, where she had once lived for many years in Le Verger, the house opposite the church. The new owners spoke to her on several occasions, finding her funny, full of life and slightly bizarre. Elsa would often be seen walking between the village and the town, wandering, using up her time. The funny English bag lady with the balding wig.

The summers were good there, and during those warm dry days she would go for walks along the River Seine and watch the boats sail past. The English boats would remind her of the home country she had left so long ago. Reminding her, ironically, that she was becoming more forgetful; even English words were becoming harder to recall when she needed them. She was forgetting where she put her things and her possessions had started to get lost.

In 1983, Peter Cotterell had written to Elsa, letting her know that her sister, Joan, his mother, had died. She replied with such melancholy and retrospect – twice. Having lost the first letter, she wrote a second; and, upon finding the original, sent both. She was not close to her sister at this point, but there was significance to her feelings. She had lost other siblings before.

In stark realisation of the consequence of her younger sister's death, she wrote, '*I am the only one left.*'

There was so much more meaning to this short sentence, and though Elsa did not enlarge upon the statement, it seems certain that as she wrote those few words, she was reflecting upon her childhood. There was a burden from that time that had sat upon her shoulders, largely unspoken, all those years. A survivor's guilt possibly lived inside her during her many years and guided her path. An irrational feeling that she had survived things others had not, and it did not make sense.

During her long life, Elsa Mathiot, the outsider, had faced loneliness, rejection and sidelining. Elsa was, however, a natural survivor and, surprisingly, an outwardly jovial spirit, who enjoyed conversation and jokes, and who valued the contact she had with her nephew Peter. She also harboured a huge secret that walked beside her throughout her entire long life. Maybe that is why she left England and went to France. Maybe that is why she had no children of her own. To survive, she needed to put distance between herself and the haunting events.

She died in Vernon Hospital on 3rd January, 1989, aged ninety-two. She had quietly carried the burden with her since she was nine years old. A burden that was heavier than her carrier bag of possessions, and one that stayed with her when she lost her handbag or forgot things.

Elsa had been a mischievous child, earning her the description and name of 'Monkey'. The family always referred to her as such, and she always mentioned it in her letters. Her given name had been Elsie, but she had changed that to Elsa before she moved to France. More European, more *avant-garde*.

'*I am also known as Monkey,*' she wrote when signing off her letters to Peter and his wife, Barbara. We will generally refer to her as Monkey, and, when fitting, Elsa.

It is not entirely clear how much Peter Cotterell knew about the events that Monkey had endured. He had known a little about the murders, but later he discovered more specific details. Accounts differ in relation to what conversations he had had with whom. With the discovery, the difficulties in the relationship with his mother perhaps became easier, though no less painful, to understand. His unhappy childhood and that of his sister, Pamela, was not one they wanted to impose upon children of their own, and both resolved to raise happy, loving families, in distinct contrast to their own background. In so doing, they broke the short cycle, but the partial knowledge of the events still hung over the family like a fog. Peter knew he had been named after his grandfather, but later discovered that Peter Robert Head was the cause of the family problems. His grandfather, who had been so affectionately spoken of, was, in fact, one of the biggest mass murderers of children, and most likely the biggest in the history of the Wiltshire Constabulary, which investigated the case.

The case created headlines across Great Britain and Ireland, then promptly became chip paper. There was no mystery to keep the public guessing as to who committed the crime, and there was no one to hang. The story did not get buried, it just dropped out of local consciousness. That is, except for the family who had to live under the substantial shadow it left, along with the single lingering mystery as to why it had occurred.

CHAPTER 2

Peter Robert Head Enters the World

I n contrast with the many siblings his own children would
have, Peter Robert Head was that Victorian rarity, an
only child.

His parents, Peter, a Wiltshire man who grew up in the
more salubrious confines of the Salisbury Cathedral Close,
and Elizabeth, née Fisher, a London girl, had met while
working in service in Winchester in Hampshire. Peter had
left Wiltshire to work as a valet and coachman for the family
of George Meredith Wallace, a former Captain in the 16th
Regiment of Foot, in Harford House on the Isle of Man. Also
living there was Wallace's father, Peter Wallace, who had
risen to the rank of General in the Royal Artillery. Elizabeth
had grown up in Judd Street, Bloomsbury, where her father
ran a tailoring business. By sixteen, she was in service in St
Pancras, working for the family of James Osbourne Struthers,
a Scottish solicitor.

Peter and Elizabeth were both living at The White Hart,
Winchester, when they married on 16th December, 1856.
Maria Wing, Peter's sister, and her husband, John, were
witnesses at their wedding, which was held at St Maurice's
Church in the centre of the cathedral city.

With both being experienced in hospitality, running a
pub was the ideal joint venture for the newly-married Peter
and Elizabeth Head. Conveniently for them, in 1857 the

latest in a series of domestic violence assaults led to the imprisonment of the landlord of the St James Tavern in Winchester, and consequently the availability of the landlord liquor licence. Peter and Elizabeth snapped up the chance to fulfil their dream, and, after securing a glowing reference from a local brushmaker, John Wing, who also happened to be his brother-in-law, Peter persuaded the magistrates that he was an upstanding member of the community who deserved to hold the licence. The application conveniently forgot to mention Peter's conviction of drunk and disorderly and assaulting a police officer in Salisbury a few years earlier. Out drinking in the city with his brother, Robert, they had got into a fight and later violently resisted arrest. The two brothers and another friend who had grown up with them in Cathedral Close were lucky to escape with fines, but the behaviour did not seem conducive with boys growing up under the magnificence of the Salisbury Cathedral and the incident was probably the catalyst that caused them to move away.

Peter and Elizabeth's son, Peter Robert Head, was born on 4th September, 1858, in their living quarters upstairs at the St James Tavern.

The baby was only ten days old when, on Tuesday, 14th September, his uncle, Robert William Head, married Mary Ann Pearce in St Maurice's Church in the centre of Winchester.

Peter and Robert's mother, Miriam, took the opportunity to travel from her home in the shadow of Salisbury Cathedral to Winchester, both to meet her new grandchild and attend her son's wedding. Miriam's daughter, Maria, and her husband, John Wing, again acted as witnesses, and there was a small Head family gathering at the St James Tavern to wet the head of baby Peter Robert Head and celebrate Robert's marriage.

The day after the wedding, Elizabeth was upstairs in the living quarters of the pub, tending to eleven-day-old Peter Robert.

Miriam Head was sitting quietly having a drink in the public bar of the St James Tavern. Punters were dotted around the public bar, drinking their ale or port and warming themselves from the increasingly cooling outdoors. Peter was serving behind the bar when a local troublemaker, William Hogger, who was a diminutive and garrulous character and had that very day been released from prison, came into the St James Tavern, already drunk, and soon started practising his speciality. He was drinking with another man when the conversation became argumentative, before predictably descending into a fight. Peter had already shown he was no shrinking violet when it came to physical confrontation. However, he was now not in the best of health, which, together with consideration of his liquor licence, obliged him to take a cautious approach with this hooligan, whom he had undoubtedly encountered before. He also had the welfare of his customers to think of, not least of whom was his elderly mother, Miriam. The presence upstairs of his new baby and the absence of his stronger brother may also have been decisive factors in his decision to try a more malleable approach, rather than utilising the violence he had been convicted of in Salisbury.

Peter vainly attempted to appeal to the despicable William Hogger to calm down. Hogger, who articulated even more vocabulary with his fists than his mouth, laid into Peter with his lifetime experience of violence. Chairs and tables went flying and two of the pub windows were broken. Peter was forced to leave the pub to find a policeman and did so very quickly in the form of Police Constable Pithers. Whilst Peter was gone, however, Hogger turned his attention to Miriam, tearing off her bonnet and punching the old lady several times in the head.

A one-armed man called John Waters had just entered the pub as the dishevelled old woman was sprawled across the table, with her bonnet trodden into the sawdust-covered floor. Waters utilised his remaining arm and pulled Hogger off Miriam, only to be punched in the face himself, sustaining a very black eye. He was no match for Hogger's drunken aggression. Peter returned with PC Pithers, who gained the better of Hogger, arrested him and dragged him out of the pub towards the police station. On the way, the wily and violent Hogger managed to break loose and assault the officer, before being subdued once again as an off-duty soldier came to PC Pithers' aid. Even in court the following day, Hogger maintained an air of verbal aggression, and he was given sixty-three days in custody as well as having to pay for the damage to the windows in the pub.

Such was the environment over the next three years, where punters regularly lost their ability to walk and talk, that young Peter Robert Head acquired his.

In 1861, possibly as a result of these circumstances or possibly owing to Peter's failing health, he and Elizabeth decided to leave the pub business and return to her native London. In May, they probably attended the funeral of Peter's father, Robert, in Salisbury Cathedral. A yeoman who had lived more than thirty years in Cathedral Close, Robert was afforded the honour of being buried within the Cathedral cloisters. At the funeral, young Peter Robert would have been reunited briefly with his grandmother, Miriam, and his grandfather's brother, great uncle Peter, who lived in Bournemouth.

Elizabeth Head's parents and brothers, the Fisher family, had latterly lived in Everett Street, Bloomsbury. During the late 1850s, William Fisher had become unable to continue working as a tailor, perhaps because of failing eyesight. He moved his wife and younger son, Thomas, to Norwood, where they took a residence in Crystal Terrace. William secured employment as an assistant at the Crystal Palace and Thomas worked as a waiter.

With the plethora of hospitality jobs evolving at the magnificent new Crystal Palace, that area was the natural place for Peter and Elizabeth to settle, and Peter secured a job as a waiter. They lived in Leather Bottle Lane, not half a mile from Elizabeth's parents and brother.

Peter Head did not last particularly long in the waiter's job. The poor health that may have precipitated their move to London was Bright's disease, a term for a collection of ailments involving the kidneys. In the days before dialysis, Peter was condemned to an early but prolonged and painful death from the time the vomiting, headaches, pericarditis and seizures took hold. Peter Robert, aged nearly eight years old, helplessly watched his father's deterioration. On 29th August, 1866, at their home in Leather Bottle Lane, Elizabeth was with Peter when, only forty years old, he took his last breath. He was buried three days later at All Saints Church, Upper Norwood. Elizabeth's own father, William, died the following year, and she was now left to fend for herself and Peter Robert, who was still too young to help the household.

Life was always difficult for a working-class Victorian widow. The choices were few: remarry; find work and leave your child; starve; or go to the workhouse. Elizabeth would never remarry, but she knew she could work if she did not have the burden of the child.

Elizabeth remained in London and certainly by the time of the 1871 census, had secured employment in Grosvenor Square as a 'Lady's maid' for the family of George John

Milles, Lord Sondes, a Baron who was a veteran of the Battle of Waterloo and had been present at the coronation of Queen Victoria. Such work, however, necessitated giving her young son into someone else's care.

CHAPTER 3

Peter Grows Up

Elizabeth had maintained contact with the Head family's Wiltshire and Hampshire contingents. Miriam still lived in Cathedral Close in Salisbury and her brother-in-law, Peter, lived in Bournemouth.

It is likely at the point when Elizabeth started work for the Milles family that Peter was initially sent to his grandmother in Salisbury. However, Miriam Head died in 1869. She was buried near to her husband in Salisbury Cathedral grounds. Two small square stones, marking both their burials, can still be seen in the middle of the Cathedral cloisters known as the Cloister Garth.

With his mother working, his grandmother now dead, and his uncle Robert busy with his own family in Lyndhurst, Peter was sent further south. He may have been left in the charge of the brother of his late grandfather, great uncle Peter, who lived in St John's Wood Road (subsequently renamed Saint Swithun's Road), Bournemouth, not far from St Peter's Church. Regardless of whose charge he was in, the eleven-year-old Peter Head was then sent to this nearby church and accepted as a chorister, a position which came with schooling and boarding.

Peter boarded with several other boys around his age in a house in Oxford Street, Bournemouth. There were about eighteen choristers, split between the 'Home Boys', those who lived in a newly-built choir home under the care of a matron, and the 'Town Boys', those who, like Peter, boarded in the town.

St Peter's Church was still under construction. The grand replacement for the earlier building, which came to be considered unsuitable for such a thriving and beautiful town, was being built in stages to manage the cost, and would not be finished until 1879. The build was being managed by the first vicar of St Peter's, Reverend Alexander Morden Bennett. It was a slow process, dependent upon available funds. Bennett was not in a hurry: he had a vision and knew what he wanted for the main church of this thriving seaside town. Even while only partially built, many concerts were held there. The choir of boys was, from 1869, led very ably by the talented Thomas Burton, who probably would have had a far brighter musical career had he not chosen to remain so dedicated to Bournemouth.

With the other choristers, Peter was educated at St Peter's School, next to the church. The young choristers' duties consisted of singing Evensong every day, the Litany on Wednesday and Friday, and a total of four services each Sunday.

Rev. Bennett was a strict disciplinarian, and Burton, having initially found him austere, soon discovered that Bennett was a very well-respected member of the town's community and was received like the town patriarch, knowing most people by their name.

So it was that by the age of thirteen, Peter Robert Head was devoid of immediate family, being separated from his mother and living in a disciplined institution; an institution that told him where to be and when to go, what to do and what to wear. As he entered puberty, he was living in a strict patriarchy, disciplined, no doubt, with regular reference to the hand of God.

The continual and gradual expansion of the church took place around him, and Peter was there during the installation of a new organ and peal of new bells. It is more than possible that he also joined the Volunteer Rifle Corps at an early age, as Rev. Bennett took a great interest in that organisation, having been involved in its foundation.

In 1874, Peter's great uncle Peter died in Bournemouth. He was buried at Canford Magna Church. It was around this time that Peter, aged around sixteen and with a deepening voice, returned to London to his mother Elizabeth, carrying with him a religious respect, an institutionalised view of life, and an incipient love for singing and performing.

In 1881, Elizabeth Head was still a Lady's maid, boarding in a house in Halsey Terrace in Chelsea. Also boarding there was a younger French lady who was a dressmaker, and it may well be from her that Elizabeth started to learn the skill of dressmaking, which she used to make a living later in life.

Peter found work as a butler in the St George's Square home of James Giffard, a retired Captain of the Madras Army. Giffard had been a surgeon in the army and had done very well for himself subsequently. Although in the latter years of a life which only had three years remaining, it may well be the case that James Giffard inspired Peter Robert Head to join the army, or at least added to the stories about General Meredith that Peter had heard from his father and the encouragement he'd received from Rev. Bennett.

Seeing there was more to be gained from the world than a life of domestic service, Peter joined up.

CHAPTER 4

Becoming a Soldier

At twenty-two years old, Peter had not grown to be a big man. He stood at 5 feet 5 inches, weighed 8 stone 8 lb, and had a 34-inch chest. He had a thin face with a fairly long nose under his mop of wavy dark brown hair, and his grey eyes were bright and engaging.

On 25th January, 1882, Peter walked into the recruiting office at Woolwich and signed up to the Royal Artillery. Although feeling the need to give his age as twenty-two and four months instead of his real twenty-three years, he was examined and declared fit.

After undertaking his training with 5th Brigade, on 1st April he was transferred to 3rd Brigade, and on 9th August, 1882, not long into his army career, together with his colleagues, he boarded a troop ship and sailed for Egypt. This young man, who had lived in the rural counties and dirty capital city of England, was about to see more of the world.

The 1869 opening of the Suez Canal had dramatically reduced the journey time for British shipping bound for the Indian Ocean, and, as such, it was an important strategic resource for Britain. Civil strife had erupted in Egypt, causing a change of regime, and the relationship between Egypt and Britain started to deteriorate. Eager to reinstate their ally, the Khedive, as ruler of Egypt, and thereby ensure their continuing use of the Suez Canal, in July, 1882, the British invaded what remained of Alexandria, after a two-day naval bombardment. The eventual battle of Tel-el-Kebir took place in September, 1882, and the Artillery was very much a part of this decisive action. This was a baptism of fire for Peter. With very little real training before he left for Egypt, he would have had to adapt and learn very quickly. The horrors of war would have been all around him. It is difficult to know precisely what part Peter played in the battle, but, as a driver in the Artillery, it would have been a significant part, and he would have been present at the most difficult times for the Artillery, as well as seeing the resulting carnage of their bombardment when they advanced. For his part, Peter was awarded the Tel-el-Kebir clasp to the Queen's Sudan Medal, as well as the Khedive's Star. Peter remained in Egypt until 27th April, 1883, when he returned to England.

Later, newspapers across the country would report erroneously that Peter suffered from severe sunstroke while he was serving with the Artillery in India. There are, however, no medical records remaining in his military history. If it did happen, it most certainly occurred in Egypt, as this appears to be his only foreign military posting.

Regardless of any sickness he experienced, he must have performed well in his role in Egypt, for on his return he was promoted from Driver to Bombardier. In August, 1885, Bombardier Head was promoted to Corporal and sent on a six-week gunnery course. On 24th April, 1886, he was promoted to Sergeant, and with that promotion came a new mess, new messmates, and an altogether better standard of life and entertainment.

CHAPTER 5

First Marriage

Whilst Peter was settling into his life as a Sergeant of the Royal Artillery and enjoying the benefits of the Sergeants' Mess and military life in peaceful England, across the country in Chatham, Kent, Amy Matilda Tanner worked as a housemaid in the household of Frank Varley, the curate of St Paul's in Chatham. Her father was George Tanner, a Wiltshire man from the village of Great Somerford, who had started adult life as a thatcher and a carpenter, but then joined the Royal Engineers as a musician and brought up his family in Chatham, largely in Brompton Barracks. One of thirteen children, Amy grew up surrounded by the army. On Peter's return from Egypt, he may have been in Chatham for a while, or maybe it was on his gunnery course; regardless, their paths crossed.

Peter and Amy were married on 11th April, 1887, in Brompton Parish Church.

In November, 1887, Sergeant Head was transferred to the newly formed 10th Battery of the 1st Brigade Lancashire Division, and although it was part of the Lancashire Brigade, 10th Battery was posted to his home county of Hampshire. Peter and Amy were provided with married quarters in Fort Grange, Gosport, and it was here on 28th February, 1888, that their daughter, Amy Edith Head, was born.

Domestic happiness was even shorter for Peter than it had been for his mother. Baby Amy Edith Head was less than a year old when, on 7th February, 1889, her mother died. Amy Matilda had contracted pulmonary tuberculosis – phthisis as it was then known. It was a horribly ubiquitous and contagious disease that people succumbed to after becoming rattling and coughing skeletal shadows of their former selves. Peter was a helpless bystander as Amy held on for eight months whilst the disease sucked the life from her. He was present at their barracks home of 8 Ottawa Terrace when his twenty-five-year-old wife died.

Losing his wife, being left with a baby while living in barracks, and having a job to do were not the only problems Peter faced. Amy Matilda had left something else for their daughter. Little Amy Edith had also contracted tuberculosis. Hers manifested differently, and before she was eighteen months old her left leg had to be amputated in order to save her life. The only solution for Amy's welfare was to send her to her maternal grandparents, the Tanners. George Tanner had retired from being a musician in the army, but stayed living in Kent, where he made a living as a carpenter. With these skills he made his young grand-daughter her first crutches. Two of his sons were also carpenters. George did not live long enough to build Amy more crutches as she grew; he died later that same year. Amy remained in the care of her grandmother, Fanny Tanner, and lived at their home in Old Brompton, sharing with her aunts and uncles, while her father pursued his regular army, and started an irregular performing career.

CHAPTER 6

Bachelor Again

Now a widower, Sergeant Peter Head was moved to the barracks in Wareham, Dorset, where he threw himself into mess life. Despite the personal grief he had experienced, as a man Peter had thrived living in a disciplined institution. His growth in confidence and ability to find his own personality in an environment that mostly tried to remove the notion of individuality enabled him to begin once again to indulge himself in the passion he had acquired for singing in public. He also noticed how satisfying it was to hear the laughter at the comic songs he sang. Like his voice, his life experience was now deeper. The layers of trauma were slowly settling upon his shoulders. As a chorister, he had lost his father and been sent away by his mother. As a soldier, on top of what he saw serving in the Egyptian war, he had now lost a wife and had to leave his daughter after seeing her go through the trauma of an amputation so young.

Life became less reverent, and Peter took the opportunity to perform for his colleagues in the mess and, increasingly, on stage. The material performed was also substantially different from what he would have sung in St Peter's Church, Bournemouth, and certainly not anything of which Rev. Alexander Morden Bennett would have approved. Peter became a very active entertainer, learning and performing a number of popular comedy routines and songs. At every given opportunity, Sergeant Head became the entertainment.

Officers joining or leaving the Battery were always good reasons for a knees-up, and such postings were regular occurrences. Peter's performances were a popular booking. As an example, in October, 1889, Peter provided the comic entertainment at the leaving party for Sergeant Major Blackmore in the Sergeants' Mess in Weymouth.

The following year, he performed much of the entertainment at a 'smoking concert' at the barracks. His turns were often singled out for special praise, and he became a very popular member of the Battery who was sought after to provide the entertainment. Particularly in the mess, his jovial performances would have lifted the rather tedious and mundane nature of a soldier's life when not at war. The soldiers and non-commissioned officers of the Artillery loved Sergeant Head and his comic songs, and Sergeant Head loved performing them. The levity of this army life, and the demand he received as an entertainer, provided an antidote and distraction to the heartache he had just personally experienced.

To celebrate New Year, 1892, a series of smoking concerts was held in the 'Red Room' at the barracks in Weymouth on 3rd, 4th and 5th January. The doors were also open to the many members of the local community who battled their way through the wind and rain to join the Artillery at the event. There were many acts on the programme, and Peter was amongst those giving such great performances as to merit an encore and a mention in the newspaper. He participated in the entire process and was part of the stage management team, as well as carrying out the construction of the stage.

Peter Robert Head was now not just a sergeant in the Artillery, he was somebody. He was well known, a big celebrity in his small world, and a new lady was about to enter his life.

CHAPTER 7

Florence and More Little Heads

Florence Ellen King was to become a doomed mother. A woman who would endure the weight of extreme grief into extreme old age, she was the epitome of resilience, who practised the art of Victorian stoicism well into the twentieth century.

Florence was born on 14th March, 1871, to James and Emily King. At the time of her birth, James was working as a night foreman on the railway and the family was living in Regent Street, Worcester. Florence was the fifth of their eleven children. By 1881, the family had moved to Melbourne Terrace, Worcester, and James was working for the Great Western Railway as a foreman. What did come with so many children was a lack of space, and the older children moved out as soon as they could. Florence's eldest brother, James Bryan King, had joined the army, and in 1886 married while serving in Jersey. Her brother, Albert, had also married and moved to Weymouth, Dorset. By her late teens, Florence had left the family home for a job in service and, with the requirement to make her own way in life, her resilience began to build. Though she didn't know it, she would need to absorb all the strength she could.

In 1891, Florence was living in Westbury-on-Trym near Bristol and working at a house called The Larches. Here, Florence had the relatively unique Victorian insight of experiencing life in a matriarchal household devoid of male influence. She worked as parlour maid to an eighty-six-year-old lady called Ellen Braysher and her companion of many years, fifty-nine-year-old Amelia Ann Blanford Edwards.

When it came to the census of that year, Florence had given her age as three years older than she actually was, and perhaps she had pretended to be older in order to secure work at The Larches. Amelia Edwards was, in fact, a renowned and celebrated individual, a successful and published author of both novels and travel books. In addition, she was the first female Egyptologist and was immensely knowledgeable and influential in that field. She had undertaken much work in Egypt, before the likes of Howard Carter, the celebrated finder of Tutankhamun, had thought of it, and was a co-founder of the Egypt Exploration Fund (still in existence and now called the Egypt Exploration Society). Amelia Edwards was also completely open about her sexuality and had several open lesbian relationships, even while living as partner to Ellen Braysher for over thirty years. There is no doubt that regardless of how long Florence King lived and worked here with these remarkable women, she would have sensed and seen the real potential of women's place in a world that still did not allow them the vote. In Amelia Edwards, she would have seen a great deal of strength and individualism.

Ellen Braysher died in January the following year. Amelia had moved to Weston-super-Mare in the hope the sea air would help her pneumonia, but she died later that same year. They are buried together in St Mary's Church, Westbury-on-Trym, and such is their importance, particularly in early LGBT history, that their grave is a listed monument.

It is likely that Florence King then went to stay with her brother, Albert, who was living in Newberry Street, Weymouth. This was a third of a mile from the Red Barracks where a certain Sergeant Head of the Royal Artillery was based, and with his concerts in the town, and their proximity, it seems certain that Florence Ellen King met Peter Robert Head in Weymouth.

In March, 1893, a concert was held in Peter's honour, on account of him being posted away from Dorset. Speeches were given thanking him for his service and comradeship and wishing him luck with his transfer and promotion to the permanent staff of the Sussex Artillery in Eastbourne. A toast to his honour was taken, and the night finished with him singing 'Emancipation Day'.

Peter moved to Eastbourne and took up residence in the barracks at Seaside Road. He was straight into the concert halls. In June, 1893, he was part of a 'cigarette concert' which took place at the Club Hotel, Pevensey Road, Eastbourne. The occasion was to honour a local man made good. Alfred Upperton, who had seen some success in the Lyric Theatre in London with his strong baritone voice, sang several songs, then Sergeant Head performed popular comic songs of the time. Peter Head's songs were received with great delight by the audience, which demanded several encores. This was not a military event, and Peter was the only performer credited with any rank. It therefore records a first for him, venturing as a performer outside the confines of military-arranged events. He was flourishing both professionally and, having built a new life with a new lady, personally.

Florence became Florence Ellen Head in December, 1893. Peter had obtained leave to marry, and the ceremony took place in St Clement's Church, Dulwich. Peter was thirty-five, although the marriage certificate puts him at thirty-two; Florence was twenty-two, but reported as twenty-three. Ages were never a thing to worry about then.

Florence had been staying at 8 Henslowe Road, Dulwich, close to her sister, Fanny Elizabeth Huckesby, who, with her second husband Charles, witnessed the marriage of Peter and Florence. On their marriage certificate, Peter's father is erroneously recorded as 'Robert'. Interestingly, when Fanny had married Charles Huckesby, she was a twenty-eight-year-old widow. However, their certificate records her as a spinster, and to reinforce the lie she reported her father's name as James Fudger, her late father-in-law, not James King, her actual father. Presumably, Charles Huckesby did not want it known, or perhaps did not know himself, that his new wife had been married before. It was relatively easy to cover up the documentary chronology of one's life in those times.

It is likely that Peter's mother, Elizabeth, also attended her son's second marriage, it being held near to her in a London borough just south of the River Thames. Two years earlier, Elizabeth was lodging with the family of a dairyman in Seymour Place, Marylebone. Twenty-five years since the death of her husband, she had remained single and was working her way through life, now earning a living as a dressmaker. As Florence got to know Elizabeth, she would have realised she was once again close to a strong woman who did not rely on men to finance her life.

Peter and Florence settled into married quarters in Eastbourne, where Florence supported him in his work and his performances, helping him with stage decorations and socialising. In March, 1894, Peter performed at a smoking concert held at the Ordnance Yard, Eastbourne, which was attended by all the officers of the Sussex Artillery and several hundred of the men. Peter sang his usual comic song plus another called 'Shine Shine Moon'. The show was repeated the following week for more military and townspeople.

On 20th January, 1895, Peter and Florence Head had their first child. A daughter named Mildred Grace was born in Lewes, where Peter was serving with a detachment of the Sussex Artillery. They were living in married quarters in Grange Road, Southover, Lewes, and as they both delighted in the miracle of birth and held their baby girl, no one could ever have imagined the horrors that would end her short life.

They were fully immersed in the best kind of military life, and as the church had once done to his teenage life, the British Army dictated all parts of Peter's adult life. Peter was doing well. Professionally, he was excelling in the running of his section of soldiers, through drills on the parade ground and shooting ranges, and providing the instruction, mentoring and comradeship they needed to become the gunners the country might have to call upon one day. At the same time, he was making a name for himself as a popular comic and singer.

On 19th July the following year, another daughter, Elsie Mabel, was born in the house in Grange Road.

In March, 1897, back in Hampshire, Mary Ann Head, Peter's aunt, died at the age of sixty-five, and perhaps because of grief and infirmity, his uncle Robert William Head was admitted to the Hampshire Asylum near Fareham. He was seventy-three years old and would not leave the institution alive.

Florence would later tell the Wiltshire Coroner that Peter had had a fall from the Portsmouth ramparts, injuring his head. No other record can be found in relation to this incident, but it was likely to have happened in 1897. Florence said that the head injury he sustained had affected his personality afterwards, and this hints that, although the success he was having professionally, the regular birth of his children, and later reports of his gregarious nature give no evidence of a negative change of him, in private, he was beginning to lose a degree of bonhomie and his outlook was changing.

Around this time, Peter was promoted to Company Sergeant Major and posted to Scotland. Peter, Florence and their two very young daughters packed up their belongings and made the long train and carriage journey to Helmsdale, where he served initially, high up on the east coast of Sutherland. Florence was expecting their third child, and the journey must have been quite arduous. It is quite likely that Peter's eldest child, nine-year-old Amy Edith, also went with them. If not, then she certainly joined her father, stepmother, and half-siblings a little later. This would also have meant the financial burden of sending money to wherever she was would have ceased and helped the family purse.

Working from the Drill Hall in Helmsdale, Peter's job was instructing the 7th Company 1st Caithness (Caithness and Sutherland) Artillery Volunteers, and it was in Helmsdale that Florence delivered another daughter in December, 1897. The child was named Florence Ellen Head after her mother, but she would live for only a fraction of the time her namesake would. For the time being, the little Head children flourished in the fresh Scottish air, the older ones absorbing a slight Scottish lilt into their developing vocabulary as they played with local children. This youngest addition to their family would later be the first to be found dead.

CHAPTER **8**

The Good Soldier

With Peter's increase in rank and status, even with young children in tow, Florence became more involved in their new barracks life. Peter became a very popular instructor of the Caithness Artillery Volunteers and a well-liked member of the community. He characteristically set about becoming prominent on the concert scene. On New Year's Eve, 1897, the 7th Company held a concert at the Drill Hall, Helmsdale. This was a new audience for Peter, and his performances were received ecstatically. The *John O'Groat Journal* wrote an account of the evening and made particular reference to Peter: '*The new instructor, Sergeant Major Head, will undoubtedly prove a source of strength to his Corps. An Egyptian campaigner and rare comic to boot, he cannot but impress the boys as a good fellow.* [Sergeant Head's contribution]... *was, moreover, new to a Helmsdale audience, and so much appreciated that a second appearance became necessary to satisfy the desire for more.*' (*John O'Groat Journal* – Friday, 31st December, 1897.)

On 28th February, 1898, for the Company's annual ball, Peter and Florence worked hard together to elaborately decorate the Helmsdale drill hall with evergreens interlaced from wall to ceiling to make an arch. They painted the walls a terracotta colour. Two large stars and a crown shaped by swords adorned one wall, and the harness for the field guns was put on display. It was noted how much effort Peter and Florence had put into the event with the bunting and chandeliers. The decorations *'eclipsed previous years'*. One contemporary account said, *'It may be said that the popular instructor, Sergeant Major Head, whose indefatigable labours coupled with those of Mrs Head and some other willing hands deserve the highest praise for the care and trouble with which the hall had been transformed to its brilliant appearance for the occasion.'* (*John O'Groat Journal* – Friday, 11th February, 1898.) The evening continued with a traditional military meal and drinks, followed by speeches and dancing. As usual, it went on to 5am.

Peter performed well in training his troops in soldiering, too. In April, 1898, there was an examination of 'gun layers'. This is the art of aiming the field guns or other artillery and having control over the angle of elevation or trajectory of the fire. All the men Peter had instructed passed the examination, and two obtained maximum marks, for which Peter received great praise and credit.

On a stormy Scottish day in May, 1898, Lieutenant Colonel G. J. Playfair undertook an inspection of the Company. Owing to the weather, it was held inside the drill hall instead of on the 'Battery Field'. A careful inspection was made of the soldiers' uniforms as they stood in line. They were marched to the front of the hall and brought to attention by Sergeant Major Head and duly inspected; some were questioned about gunnery drill, and Lt Col Playfair was very impressed, telling them so, with very complimentary comments concerning Sergeant Major Head as well as the general cleanliness and smartness of the men. Peter Head was at the height of everything he could imagine was good. He excelled at work, he received praise as an entertainer, and Florence had produced a family he hadn't had himself as a child. She in turn was universally respected as his devoted assistant. The only thing that would improve his lot would be a son.

The men of Peter's company were all volunteers, meaning many were undertaking other jobs and therefore coming and going as opportunities arose. In June, 1898, Peter gave a farewell speech in the drill hall at a presentation for one of his sergeants, Fred Fraser, a fish scourer who was leaving because he had secured a position with the Fishery Board at Lerwick. In January, 1899, Peter attended the annual ball at the drill hall, which again involved dancing all night. By now, however, Peter had moved fifty miles to the north coastal town of Mey to instruct volunteers there. This was as far away as you could get from Bournemouth or Winchester in mainland Britain. It also brought Peter a new audience as well as new students.

Florence was pregnant again, but this time decided to take the long journey back south to give birth in her mother's house in Little Southfield Street, Worcester. Their first son, William Robert Head, was born on 24th June, 1899. He was most probably named after Peter's uncle, Robert William, who was still in the asylum in Hampshire. Now with a son at last, and notwithstanding the head injury Florence would speak of, Peter was quite possibly at the apotheosis of his contented life.

On 18th January, 1900, Peter arranged a Grand Concert and Assembly at the Mey drill hall which was intended to fund prizes and a picnic for all the children of the local school. In a welcome distraction from the bitter Scottish winter, Peter performed comic songs as well as a comic pantomime piece which elicited very favourable comments. At the conclusion of the performances, Peter was given a vote of thanks, and he replied with a humorous speech. The drinking and merriment then continued into the early hours. Together with a local man, George Laing, Peter's comedy act was described as '... *always a favourite with Mey audiences*'.

CHAPTER 9

The Road to Retirement

The annual ball of the Mey Artillery Volunteers in January, 1901, had to be cancelled owing to the death of Queen Victoria on 22nd January, throwing the nation into a state of mourning. The news arrived at Wick at 1900 hours that evening, only half an hour after the Queen had taken her last breath. The church clock chimed every half hour and the community, half expecting the news for a week or so, understood. All events of a happy nature were cancelled, and the only mitigation in sadness was the recognition of Queen Victoria's long life and legacy. Victoria's son, Albert Edward, became King Edward VII.

Services were held all over the country. The Mey Artillery Volunteers, under the overall command of Captain Cheyne, paraded at Mey Drill Hall. The Rev. Munro from Canisbay took a service there that was attended not only by the Volunteers, but also a substantial number of the local community. No doubt Amy was there, and the four younger Heads, Mildred, Elsie, Florence and William, too. Aware of the reverence of the occasion, they stood with their once again heavily pregnant mother, as they proudly watched their father bark orders of command for the smart parade to march and wheel.

Peter's uncle, Robert William Head, died in Hampshire in March, 1901. It is unlikely that Peter would have taken leave to attend the funeral such a long way away; besides, having someone in the family who died in a lunatic asylum was not something people highlighted. A month later, Florence and Peter had another son, Peter, who was born in their quarters in the drill hall in Mey.

Peter had now completed nineteen years of Army service. The Artillery had reorganised, and he was part of the Royal Garrison Artillery (RGA). Peter's thirteen-year-old daughter from his first marriage, Amy, was living with him and Florence and her younger half-siblings, Mildred Grace (six), Elsie Mabel (four), Florence Ellen (three), William Robert (one), and new baby Peter. Elsie Mabel Head had become a bit of a tearaway and had earned the nickname 'Monkey', which stayed with her for the rest of her life. They all lived seemingly happily in the drill hall in Mey, where Peter was now regarded as being a steady, intelligent man who paid particular attention to his duty. He was later described as having been, during those days, civil and obliging to everyone and well-liked by the Volunteers.

His involvement in the wider community extended to being very active in helping set up and run the Mey Dramatic Society, arranging concerts and plays, often to raise money to buy prizes for shooting competitions for his Volunteer RGA company. In June, 1901, the local police officer was posted away to a new role, and once again a leaving ceremony was held in the drill hall, with Peter, amongst others, giving a speech.

On Monday, 29th July, 1901, Peter's mother, Elizabeth, still forging a living as a dressmaker in London, was admitted into the infirmary of Marylebone Workhouse. She declared as sixty-nine years old, though she was never particularly precious about the veracity of her age. She was unwell, and the only recourse to medical help for those on the breadline was the workhouse. Marylebone had built a new part to their workhouse a year earlier, enabling the institution to house well over a thousand people. Despite the fact that some of the contemporary photographs still conjure thoughts of *Oliver Twist* and gruel, it was a relatively humane place to be, albeit no doubt disciplined and wanting of much in the way of affection. Peter and his mother had stayed in touch, and he had visited her regularly over the years. Upon her admission to the infirmary, Elizabeth supplied Peter's details as her next of kin, giving his address correctly as being in Mey, near Thurso, Scotland. Peter provided financial support, too, and would have received bills from the workhouse, being a man of relatively good means.

By 28th August, Elizabeth had recovered sufficiently to request to be discharged, and duly returned to her accommodation and resumed her dressmaking. Peter may well have had to help her with her rent at this time, as her work productivity was dramatically reduced.

The annual ball of the 5th Company 1st Caithness Volunteer Artillery took place on Friday, 3rd January, 1902. Sergeant Major Head '*artistically executed*' the decorations of the hall very efficiently, '*reflecting much credit*' on him. The prizes were presented for the shooting competition and a long and enjoyable evening was had by all. This time, Peter was not mentioned as partaking in the entertainment, though almost certainly he would have done so.

For the past twenty years he had not had to think about housing his family or where the next meal was going to come from. He, personally, had become a central, influential, and important part of wherever it was he had worked. Retirement was looming, and with it the prospect of having to find work and a home in which his young children could grow up.

He had had the best of army life, paying minimal, if any, rent and saving up his pay. His brief and bloody exposure to

32

warfare and global travel while he was young had given him adventure, experience, stories, and, with that, credibility. He proudly wore his Egyptian medals, and for the eighteen years of his service following the Egyptian campaign, the biggest dangers he had to face came from the potential of negligent discharges of weapons by his younger charges or falling off a stage at a concert hall. He had experienced a minor celebrity status wherever he was stationed through his gregarious and funny performances. The best of an army career was coming to an end. He needed to plan a future.

1902 was the Heads' final year in Scotland. Peter and Florence set to return to England and decided upon a rural and comparatively reclusive life in comparison with hitherto. They invested their savings in a poultry farm.

In November, 1902, Peter participated in his last recorded stage performance. It was well advertised weeks earlier and consisted of two farcical plays performed by the Mey Dramatic Society, together with the usual songs and merriment. Peter *'worked like a Trojan in connection with the several arrangements'*. He kicked off the proceedings with a rendition of 'Emancipation Day' and then the plays 'Temporary Insanity' and 'The Enquiry Office' were enacted. A borrowed gramophone was used to play a number of records to the audience, a novel thing for many. Then the finale was 'The Elephant Battery', which depicted a camp scene in India in which Peter's son, three-and-a-half-year-old William Robert, took part, armed with a hatchet and sitting upon the 'elephant'. Peter may well have watched his young son playing on stage and thought him a chip off the old block, with the exception of the young lad's mild Scottish accent. He would have certainly looked on with pride at William, and no doubt wondered about his bright future.

At the end of the performances, Peter was afforded a vote of thanks by a grateful and entertained audience. He was credited as being responsible for forming and driving the Mey Dramatic Society in the town and appears to have been the main driving force for the Society, as there was no further mention of it in the local press after Peter left Scotland.

CHAPTER 10

Soldier to Farmer

Peter and Florence had already invested their savings in a smallholding of some seven acres in an area called Picket Twenty in Andover, in Peter's home county of Hampshire. It is unclear when the notion arose, or what influenced such a move, but some time before the day of his retirement, it was a done deal. With Florence heavily pregnant once again, it is likely that, although not yet retired, the family moved to the slightly warmer climate of rural Andover well before the end of 1902.

On 3rd January, 1903, Florence gave birth to another son. Alfred was born in their new home, the farm at Picket Twenty. He was their sixth child and third son.

Back in Scotland, the Mey Volunteers held their annual ball on 23rd January, 1903. There is no record of Peter having performed, and strangely, despite all the work he did in the community, there is no mention of him leaving Mey or retiring from the Artillery. He was certainly in Scotland on the night of the ball, but seemingly did not have an involvement or a speech marking his departure. This incongruous lack of ceremony speaks of a change in his character and marks a move away from everything he had known.

On 24th January, he sat in the drill hall in Thurso with Lieutenant Colonel McDonald and signed his discharge papers. He had exactly twenty-two years' service in the

British Army and was leaving with his Egyptian Medal with the clasp, the Khedive's Bronze Star, together with his Long Service and Good Conduct medals. He now stood at 5 feet 6 inches, his chest had grown to 40 inches and his hair had naturally greyed in his latter years. He was signed off with an exemplary record and furnished with a recommendation that he would make a good clerk.

Sergeant Major Peter Robert Head of the Royal Garrison Artillery became Mr Head, chicken farmer of Andover. He walked to the train station and away from twenty-two years of being told what to do and when to do it, of being housed and fed, of regular income, of being a central part of a social and professional community; an instructor, a role model, a respected and experienced bloodied soldier, a leader of men, as well as a funny and loved entertainer to many locally.

He had left for an isolated plot of land into which his life savings were invested, intending to develop it into a profitable chicken farm. All of a sudden, the future prosperity of his family was solely in his hands.

On 7th February, 1903, he registered the birth of his fourth son, Alfred, and gave 'Poultry Farmer' as his occupation. Then, on 19th April, Alfred was baptised in St Mary's Church, Andover, again with Peter's occupation given as 'farmer'.

The hamlet of Picket Twenty was little more than an old farm that had developed into separate dwelling areas. In 1901, it was occupied by only three families. William Frederick Trickey, a carpenter, lived there with his wife and four children. Trickey had been in the Army in the 1880s and travelled with General Gordon to Khartoum. Frederick Bungay, a farm labourer, also lived there with his wife, Kezia. He had been a Royal Marine and had retired in 1879. They had only been married five years. He died in 1901, and it may be his house into which the Heads moved, along with the surrounding land. Robert Thatcher and his family also lived in Picket Twenty, where he was a shepherd.

Mildred, Elsie, and Florence were admitted into the Andover National School, and Peter set to developing a chicken business on the land they had bought. It would have been a great bonding time with his young boys as he would have been around far more often than when he was running the Caithness Volunteers. His children were now his only audience, and later, neighbours would talk of Peter often playing and joking with them. As the summer approached, it was noticed by neighbours that he was very careful of the sun, and the story later reported that he had suffered greatly with sunstroke while serving in India, developed. Which, of course, we know actually to have been Egypt.

As the months progressed, the financial situation for the Heads became increasingly difficult. Despite his resilience and considerable life experience, Peter was no businessman. The isolation may have also been a factor in a growing dissatisfaction. Peter had the additional worry of the increasing frailty of his mother in London and the need to help her financially.

Florence's father, James King, died on 12th June, 1903. He was buried in Astwood Cemetery, Worcester, and it is likely that Florence attended the funeral with one or two of the children while Peter remained at home, trying to make a go of their failing business. More train fares. James King's gravestone had the inscription, '*In loving memory of our dear father James King (GWR Loco Dept) who departed this life on June 12th, 1903, aged 66 years. Peace perfect peace.*' This gives the impression that his children clubbed together to get the stone. An entry in the death notices of the Worcestershire Chronicle reads, '*King – June 12 at Glyndon*

Villas, Southfield Street, after a long and painful illness, James, the beloved husband of Emily King.'

In less than a year of living in Andover, it was clear that circumstances were going to force Florence and Peter away from their farm. His savings, and with it his hope, had been exhausted on his efforts to make the farm profitable, and it became painfully apparent that, in order to survive, Peter had to find employment and they had to move away from their loss-making venture.

Florence had siblings dotted about the country; some back in Worcester where her mother was, one in Devon and one in Hampshire, with two brothers away with the Army, so there was a little potential support around. But Peter was his own man. He missed the military, the brotherhood, the connection, the being someone, and, now, the regular income. He missed not having to worry about how he would provide for his family.

CHAPTER 11

Return to the Army

With great heartache at the loss of his venture, his savings and no doubt substantial self-esteem, Peter did the only thing he could think of, and that was to return to the Army. They decided to move to Wiltshire, where there were military jobs. With his exemplary service record and the recommendation that he would make a good clerk, it should not be too difficult to find work.

He and Florence moved to Amesbury, a small town near Salisbury in south Wiltshire, which Peter would have known and very likely visited during his artillery days, owing to its proximity to the training grounds of Salisbury Plain. What is more, there were companies of Royal Artillery stationed at nearby Bulford.

The long-settled human presence in this area is evidenced, of course, by the nearby Stonehenge monument, which, when the Heads arrived in Amesbury, belonged to the Antrobus family. At the beginning of the twentieth century, however, Amesbury was a very transient place in many respects. Over the years, the population of the surrounding area often ebbed and flowed, dependent upon the political climate, and although regularly used for training and manoeuvres by the army for many years, it wasn't until 1902, when the government took ownership of 42,000 acres of Salisbury Plain, that there was a more permanent and substantially increased army population in the area. With this new temporary and passing mass of soldiers and their families in areas such as Bulford and Tidworth, Amesbury was required as a hub for transport and communications, and was further brought towards modernity with new railway links.

Apart from the ubiquitous military presence, the Amesbury into which the Head family had moved was a typical small, close-knit, rural and growing market town. There was, of course, the prominent presence of the Antrobus family, which had a significant and generous influence on the town's development. Until his death in 1899, Sir Edward Antrobus, the 3rd Baronet, had been omnipresent in the committees and decision-making processes, as well as having made donations of funds and land for various institutions, not least the schools.

Peter's first civilian job after failing at his own business was for the Institute at Bulford Camp. The Institute had been set up by the Bishop of Salisbury with a view to establishing a permanent Church of England soldiers' institute for the convenience and accommodation of troops that were to be located in the area. It was a place that those at training camps, militia, or volunteers could use for letter-writing, reading and recreation purposes. It was largely financially dependent upon public subscriptions and donations from those using it. In July, 1901, the Commander-in-Chief of the Army, Lord Roberts, opened a military bazaar in aid of the soldiers' institute at Bulford. With the typical authoritarian sycophancy of the time, this was reported as indicative of the deep interest Lord Roberts took in the welfare of the private soldier and how anxious he was to assist in improving their conditions. Citizens of Salisbury lined the streets to see him, and in his opening speech he expressed his belief that the Institute at Bulford would meet all the wants of the soldiers, supplying a long-felt need. The Institute was built in August, 1902, at a cost of £6000, and was formally opened by the Bishop of Salisbury.

It is hard to say exactly what role Peter performed at the Institute, but it is likely to have been clerical and administration work. The Institute itself was situated to the south of the Camp on the east side of the road running between the lines of huts. The building housed a devotional room and sanctuary, as well as a kitchen, toilets and bathrooms, a house for the caretaker and bedrooms for the men. There is no doubt that as the soldiers came and went, Peter would have regaled them with stories of Egypt and his time in the Army. He would have looked longingly into the large hall, which could hold seven hundred people with its raised platform serving as a stage for entertainment. He probably hoped that he might have felt at home in the environment, but with the myriad of regiments there, he would have soon felt the growing change and an incongruity between his extensive and their incipient experience.

He had also changed. He was now a greying man approaching his mid-forties who, to young soldiers in their teens and early twenties, came from a forgotten time.

His relevance had passed, and what seems to be significant is what did not happen. From Dorset to Sussex to Caithness, whenever Peter moved towns, he would soon appear on the military concert hall circuit and be the subject of rave newspaper reviews reporting a demand for encores of his performances. There was no entry in the newspapers reporting on Bulford and Amesbury events about his concert appearance, comic songs and the like. The Institute where he was now working actively staged performances. Maybe he was involved in arranging them, but he is not mentioned in any of the reports. Perhaps his performing mojo had been beaten from his soul with the losses he had endured. He had lost his farm and his savings, and he could see plainly that his position socially was in a completely different place from where it was just two years earlier.

This was a far bigger and busier environment than Mey. With no rank on his shoulder, no sparkle in his stardom and little money in his pocket, Peter now faded into the background of bustling military life. A former leading man, now an extra, commanding none of the respect and attention to which he had become accustomed. He was a clerk, a failed chicken farmer, with some old medals and a responsibility to house and feed his growing family and help out his ailing mother. Disappointed with how different it was for him and the lower status he experienced in the military, he decided on another try at civilian life.

CHAPTER 12

The Teacher, Doctor, Coroner, Policeman and Vicar – a Snapshot of Amesbury Society, 1904–5

A mesbury would soon be the scene of a tragedy. Its name would be splashed across the nation's headlines.

When Peter and Florence moved to Amesbury, together with young Mildred Grace, Elsie Mabel, Florence Ellen, William Robert, Peter and Alfred, all the individuals who would play a part in the aftermath of a huge tragedy were unwittingly living their lives in a society wondering what the new Edwardian era would bring.

On 4th January, 1904, their elder daughters, Mildred Grace and Elsie Mabel (Monkey) were admitted into Amesbury's relatively new school, built on land donated by the Antrobus family. The headmaster was Charles William Hallett, who was ably assisted by his wife, who also worked there as a teacher. Hallett was an experienced teacher and compassionate in the Victorian sense.

Charles Hallett could have come out of a Hardy novel. Born in 1856, he was brought up in Rampisham in the chalk downs of Dorset, where his once-labouring father, Israel, ran the King's Arms public house, which he stocked with beer he brewed. Charles had grown up in the pub, but having a far more philanthropical, temperate nature, chose teaching as a profession and became the teacher at the nearby village of Toller Porcorum, Dorset.

He had known Sarah Ellis most of his life, having grown up in the same village and being of the same age. They shared their passion for teaching and worked together in doing so. On 12th September, 1898, Charles Hallett secured the position of headmaster for the National School in Amesbury. In the first quarter they had an average attendance of fifteen boys and twenty girls. In early January, 1899, Charles had to close the school temporarily for a week whilst he returned to Dorset to attend to his brother, who subsequently died on 11th January. Upon reopening on 16th January, there were fifty-seven pupils. Attendance, or lack of it, was a constant battle for Charles and Sarah, and they would give out medals and certificates to those who attended most frequently. In December, 1899, their own daughter, Edith Eliza Hallett, received a special medal for having attended every day. Like she had a choice!

The number of children being admitted into the school did start to increase, but between thirty and fifty children were absent regularly on each day. In October, 1900, only eighteen of the ninety-eight students registered were absent, and at the end of January, 1901, on the last day of the old school building, one hundred and two children attended; their highest number to date. The new school building was occupied and the timetable changed to include religious instruction, the school now coming under the effective management of the church. The regular governmental inspections of the school gave the energetic Mr Hallett credit for improving the attendance. In March, 1901, an epidemic of measles broke out, which resulted in only sixty-seven of the hundred and fourteen children registered actually attending. In order to prevent the epidemic getting worse, Charles shut the school for a fortnight. The following month there was an outbreak of mumps amongst children living in the local workhouse, and they were forbidden to attend the school. By March, 1902, one hundred and five children were supposed to be attending. Illness, however, was a constant and consistent element of town life, and in October, 1902, it was diphtheria which was preventing the attendance of many children, followed by chickenpox a month later.

On 28th January, 1904, one hundred and twenty-two children managed to get into school despite the cold and the very heavy rain in the morning. Mildred and Elsie Head were very late and did not get a mark for attendance that morning. Perhaps some chaos in the Head household had delayed them.

In March, mumps again spread across the town, and several children were unable to attend school. In September that year, a very bad cough was doing the rounds, and one particular class was not allowed to perform its drill lessons, which were replaced by grammar, much to the pupils' collective chagrin. All the while, the mumps continued to multiply and increasingly contributed to the poor attendance.

There were a couple of doctors' surgeries in Amesbury, and, of course, being before the establishment of the National Health Service, all were run on private terms. As we have seen from the school records, illness could take hold of a small town very quickly, and the doctors were busy people.

The doctor Peter would use in his subsequent work was Gerard Edward Lockyer, and they would get to know each other well. Lockyer's father had been the Deputy Commissary in the Commissariat and Transport Department of the British Army. Gerard had been born in Cornwall in 1869. His father died in 1877 and Gerard went on to attend Christ's Hospital School, a boarding school in London. He was first registered as a doctor on 4th August, 1893, with a MRCS (Eng) and LRCP (Lond), having qualified at Guy's Hospital, London.

In 1900, he travelled to South Africa. If his purpose for travelling there was to look after his ailing twenty-three-year-old brother, Herbert Charles Lockyer, who was a Sergeant in the British South African Police and suffering with enteric fever in Bulawayo, Gerard arrived too late, as his brother died just weeks before Gerard travelled. Once out there, however, this being the height of the Second Boer War, Gerard became a civilian surgeon in the South African Field Force, where he was given the rank of Captain. Having spent exactly a year in South Africa, he decided to return to England. Working within the military must have influenced him in finding his way to Amesbury, where he arrived around April to settle back into civilian life. He was now decorated with the Queen's South Africa Medal and Laing's Nek clasp. When he started practising in Amesbury he was thirty-two years old and unmarried, a status that remained for the rest of his life. His South African experience would have been brutal, exposing him to many horrific and infected injuries. Dr Lockyer brought with him experience in the field of combat and a sound knowledge of post-mortem investigations.

Any coroner valued the experience and knowledge held by Dr Lockyer and relied on both when coming to conclusions in the many death inquests they held. The coroner for Salisbury and Amesbury in 1905 was the solicitor, Richard Arthur Wilson.

Richard Arthur Wilson was born in 1845, and his father, Richard Monkhouse Wilson, had been Wiltshire Coroner for the Salisbury area since 1843. In 1870, Wilson senior resigned from the role with the intention of pursuing election to the Salisbury Council. Young Richard Arthur Wilson, who was only twenty-five and already a qualified solicitor, was duly nominated to succeed his father. There was great debate in the Council Chamber of the Salisbury City Council as to this succession. The councillors argued with much feeling on the merits of having either a solicitor or a medical man in the role of coroner. Alderman John Alfred Lush, MP, provided persuasive arguments for the latter and passionately warned of the dangers of nepotism. John Lush was, of course, biased on the subject, being a physician himself and running the Fisherton Anger Lunatic Asylum alongside his civic duties.

As a result of Mr Lush's intervention, Doctor Edward Young, a forty-one-year-old Surrey man who had lived in Salisbury some ten years, was additionally nominated, and after much discussion a vote was held, from which Dr Young was narrowly elected. However, the new coroner was not a particularly healthy man himself and it was necessary to appoint a deputy in 1873. Richard Arthur Wilson was appointed to this role with less of an emotional debate than had taken place previously. He enthusiastically took on a lot of Dr Young's workload, and his first adjudication was one of accidental death on the body of a Susan Newbury, from Maiden Bradley, who burned to death in her kitchen after her clothes were set on fire from her open stove.

The role of coroner changed hands a couple more times, generating similar debates, before it briefly returned to Wilson senior, who had already lived a long life of public service, including a term as Mayor of Salisbury and myriad other civil offices. On Thursday, 26th April, 1883, he was in the Chapter House of Salisbury Cathedral, addressing a meeting of the Diocesan Synod with a speech on temperance and, more specifically, the merits of Sunday closing. Having completed his moral polemic on the evils and dangers of alcohol, he collapsed and was dead before hitting the ground. He was buried the following week in the Cathedral Cloisters just yards away from where he died. The following month, Richard Wilson wrote an open letter to the Council offering his services as Coroner and was finally appointed as such. Having already presided over the investigations of the deaths of old and young, whether natural, accidents on farms, on roads or in houses, suicides by hanging or by throat cutting, or murder, he was more than ready for the substantive role. As industrious in civil life as his father had been, Richard also held several other positions in the city, such as secretary of the Conservative Club and honorary secretary of the Salisbury Constitutional Union and Working Men's Association.

We meet Richard Arthur Wilson when he was in his late fifties. In 1881, he had married Ellen Trevenen Adams, and together they had eight children, the last of whom was born in 1896, the same year as Peter's daughter Elsie (Monkey).

Walter James Scott was the Police Sergeant of Amesbury in 1904. He was thirty-eight years old. The son of a baker, he had been a Wiltshire police officer since he was twenty-one, the year he had also married Mary Ann Tilley in Preshute, his home village. He started his police career in Trowbridge, then went to Marlborough, before performing the role of village constable for Grittleton for eighteen months and winning the respect of that community. In January, 1901, he was promoted to Sergeant and posted to Amesbury.

One of Scott's young constables was James Henry William Wells. Son of a foundry worker, Wells had grown up in Devizes and joined the police in 1900. He was a keen cricketer and would captain the police team. Amesbury was his first posting, and in 1905 he was twenty-four years old.

The vicar of Amesbury was the Reverend Reginald Fawkes. Peter would like talking to Rev Fawkes, and both had in common the fact that they had only recently settled in Amesbury. Whether or not Rev Fawkes found Peter to be the man of God he would have expected from a former chorister brought up in a church environment, or a coarse former soldier, we will not know, but Peter felt the warmth from him that was equally felt across the town. Rev Fawkes was fifty-four years old and had been ordained in 1883, holding a curacy at Paddington before becoming the chaplain of Spondon in Derbyshire, as well as spending some time as Chaplain of San Remo.

In 1890, while he was the Vicar of Spondon, he lost his first wife, Elizabeth Janet Waldegrave, daughter of the Canon of Salisbury, with whom he had a daughter. The following year, Fawkes married Elizabeth Smith, daughter of Henry Able Smith of Wilford House, Nottinghamshire, at St Martin-in-the-Fields Church, London. In 1893, he became the vicar of Canford Magna in Dorset. He had two brothers, one of whom was Colonel Lionel Grimston Fawkes, who served in the Royal Artillery for thirty-one years and retired in 1901. He had spent much of his career in the West Indies and the last two in Portsmouth, when Peter Head was serving in Scotland. It is unlikely, then, that Peter Head met Lionel in their chronologically parallel Artillery journeys, but this common link was no doubt something that educated some conversation between former Sergeant Major Peter Robert Head and the new vicar of Amesbury.

Also undertaking deacon duties in Amesbury was Algernon Charles Mainwaring Langton, the twenty-six-year-old son of Bennet Rothes Langton of Langton Hall, Langton, Lincolnshire.

On settling in Amesbury, Peter Head, as a retired Sergeant Major of the Artillery, became a member of the 28th Brigade Mess in Bulford, and there he met with the incumbent Sergeant Major of the 122nd Battery 28th Brigade Royal Field Artillery. This was Henry Crossman Stamp. Their paths may have passed briefly when Peter was in the Artillery, but their experience was very different. Peter would consider Stamp to be one of his closest friends, albeit it seems unlikely that they had even met each other outside of the mess.

Peter had seen the horrors of real battle in Egypt at Tel-el-Kebir in 1882, and then for the rest of his career enjoyed the comparative comforts, society, safety and security that came with barrack life, and, additionally, enjoying them with his growing family. In Henry Stamp he found someone who he could relate to, though with typical British soldierly stoicism of the time, it is unlikely they would have discussed their true feelings and probably bottled up any trauma they felt. Stamp may well have considered Head's career comparatively comfortable compared with his own, if indeed they did discuss their respective experiences. Being devoid of any direct reference to Peter's actual experience in Egypt, it is worth understanding what Stamp went through to imagine some of their mess-room conversations later.

At the same time as the jollities of the Caithness Artillery Volunteers' ball were being enjoyed and Sergeant Major Peter Head was relishing his latest celebrity success and adoration, Sergeant Major Henry Crossland Stamp was in the middle of the far more brutal and balanced war raging between the British and the Boers in South Africa. He had been at the Battle of Colenso, and after a narrow escape wrote to his parents ...

> '*Dear father and mother, just a few lines to let you know that I am still in the land of the living. Which is a wonder after Friday's engagement* [meaning the battle of Colenso] *we left our campground at 3:35 a.m., and received the order to advance. When about 1,000 yards from Fort Wylie, Boers opened both rifle and gunfire on us. We were in action about two hours.*

My battery [the 14th Royal Field Artillery] *worked admirably, but I think that with one or two exceptions everybody was wounded. I was hit with a portion of a shell which burst a few yards away, and left me with a beautiful black eye. The sight is not injured at all strange to say. You would remember Sergeant Grey – that tall man – well, he was shot twenty-five times, and Sergeant Howell had 13 wounds. We had six killed and 70 wounded and missing, and lost all our guns and ammunition wagons. We worked the guns as long as it was possible and a great drawback was that we could not get men to replace those who were shot at the guns. So we got the order to retire to a ditch about 20 yards away in the rear of the guns which formed good protection for us from the Boer fire. During the time the batteries were in action, the rifle fire from the Boers poured on the guns, and men fell just like rain in a thunderstorm. Sergeant Vickers is the only Sergeant left out of the 66th, and I am the only one out of the 14th with the exception of the Q.M.S who, however, is in hospital crushed, he having been so unfortunate as to have three horses shot, each of which rolled over him doing internal injuries. The Boers captured 10 guns and ammunition waggons from the two batteries – 6 belonging to the 14th and 4 from the 66th. Wishing you all a Happy and Prosperous New Year. Believe me, your affectionate son.'*

Following a deployment in Cahir, Ireland, Stamp was posted to Bulford in January, 1904, and so came to Wiltshire at a similar time as the Heads. There he lived with his wife, Clara, and three children, Clara, Harry and Arthur. Peter's conversations with Stamp certainly formed a bond between the two that at least Peter felt very strongly. Stamp's actual view on war is plain to comprehend from a sentence in a letter home to his parents after the relief of Ladysmith. '*It is nearly nineteen weeks since I left old England, but it seems like 19 years ago and I don't care how soon the war is over.*'

Peter Head's own war had really only just begun, but the foe was not to be an Egyptian or Boer; it was himself.

CHAPTER 13

The Insurance Salesman and Little Changes

In the latter part of 1904, having left work at the Institute in Bulford, Peter Robert Head started working as an agent for The Prudential Assurance Company. In this role he travelled from door to door and town to town, hoping to sell insurance, being paid a small salary boosted by commission on his sales.

It was the norm for the men of the Prudential to wear a bowler hat, and Peter, a man with all those years in uniform, welcomed and fully adopted this collective institutional dress. His hatted figure, quite likely on a bicycle at times, with a satchel containing his books, became a briefly common sight to the inhabitants of Amesbury and surrounding villages.

When he successfully persuaded clients to join the insurance scheme, he would pay a fee and arrange a meeting between the prospective client and Dr Lockyer for risk assessment purposes, and if all was well with the client's health, the deal was struck and the insurance premium paid. Peter's outwardly genial and self-assured manner helped him secure clients, and he would also go to the barracks in Bulford, knowing soldiers were a good source of business. He visited the barracks three or four times a week to collect premium payments, and this enabled him to visit the Sergeants' mess and relive his Army days over a pint or two with soldiers who had much more experience than those he had mixed with in his days at the Institute. That they were of his old regiment, too, would have bolstered that comradeship and belonging. But Peter didn't fit in completely; he dressed differently, he was older, he was an outdated outsider, who, while trying still to belong, also needed these men to buy his insurance. His head gave him grief and his anguish grew.

In June, 1904, Mildred and Elsie were suffering with chickenpox and did not attend school. No doubt the younger children caught it, too, and there followed an uncomfortable few weeks in the Head household. In September, 1904, Peter moved the family to Avon Villa in Durrington, a village two and a half miles north of Amesbury. Florence was heavily pregnant again. Mildred, Elsie, Florence, William and young Peter were enrolled in the small school in Durrington, leaving just Alfred being cared for at home. In December, 1904, Florence gave birth to their fourth son, Frederick George. He was baptised in Durrington Church on 29th January, 1905.

Peter and Florence now had seven children living in their small cottage. It was probably because of the lack of space that Peter's eldest daughter, Amy, was now living with Florence's brother, Albert, and his family in Portsmouth. This was, however, an additional expense for Peter, as he would have felt obliged to contribute to Amy's keep until she could earn a living of her own.

With a reasonable job and a pension, the poorer of the village may have looked at the Heads with some envy. Peter was seen regularly playing happily with his children, and he was often seen with a cheery disposition. Amidst this image, however, all was not right with him. The anguish and bitterness at the losses he had experienced in Andover and his changed position in society burned deep and started to affect his outlook.

When some business in relation to their land in Pickett Twenty had to be undertaken in February, 1905, Peter could not face returning there. The more resilient Florence travelled to Andover and conducted the relevant business, probably taking the younger children with her.

Further stress was added by Peter's elderly mother, Elizabeth, and her increasingly poor health. There was no room to bring her to his home, not that she was probably willing to move anyway, so her medical bills needed to be paid, as did her rent. She was deteriorating rapidly, and with no funds, once again became reliant on the workhouse and infirmary for her care.

Peter was experiencing head pains, but he rarely let on. Perhaps the head injury that Florence would speak of that hadn't seemed to affect him in his performing days did leave some incipient wound that festered and grew and, together with the mental strains he was feeling, started changing his outlook and judgement.

He started to doubt his own abilities, and though, as the good clerk he was, he recorded his work and financial takings well, the worry of managing money belonging to the company and struggling to manage his own finances sat heavily upon the shoulders that also held up an increasingly ailing head.

In April, 1905, Peter and Florence moved once again back to Amesbury and settled in a small, thatched cottage they rented in Earls Court Road. More cost, but they needed the space. Mildred and Monkey were readmitted into Amesbury School, this time along with their younger sister, Florence. The older of the boys started at the infants' school within the same building. Peter was juggling things, trying to get more clients, simultaneously keeping contact with his friends in the Artillery at Bulford, and also travelling to London to help his mother in the Marylebone Infirmary. She had been admitted there again in May, 1905. His Durrington address was recorded on the admission sheet, and they may well have written to him requesting a few expenses. The journeys to London meant days away from selling insurance, train tickets, lost revenue, more worries.

Back in Amesbury that May, there were others also going through stressful times. The popular vicar, Reverend Fawkes, temporarily stepped down from giving all the sermons, and his assistant, Algernon Langton, officiated in his stead. People of Amesbury saw the message on the church noticeboard letting them know that Rev and Mrs Fawkes were engaged in caring for his unwell only daughter, Janet. Nobody realised the seriousness of her illness, which only became publicly clear when Janet Dorothy Fawkes died on 28th May at the age of eighteen. It was a huge blow to Rev Fawkes, and something which would emotionally tie him and his wife to Amesbury for the rest of their lives, despite the brief time they were to remain there. Everybody knew Rev Fawkes and his family, and the funeral of his daughter was a large, sombre event for the town. The school was closed for the day and the Halletts and other teachers took children to the graveside, where some threw flowers into the grave. It is more than possible Monkey, Mildred, and young Florence were there. It is possible that Peter attended with Florence out of respect for Rev Fawkes. It would never have crossed their minds that within a matter of weeks some of those attending would be in their own coffins just yards away.

That summer, Sergeant Scott of Amesbury Police noticed changes in Peter and harboured an unactioned concern for him. Sergeant Scott had got to know Peter well over the previous two years in so much as a police officer should with those in his community and, in those days, could. He had had several conversations with him, and no doubt Peter had tried to sell him insurance; after all, a policeman's lot can be a dangerous one, and how would his wife and children fare should a tragedy occur? Sergeant Scott had noticed a change in Peter's outlook. He had become quiet and dejected, and even when holding a conversation with the Sergeant he was quite different from his former jovial, confident self. Peter was not displaying anything insane, and there was no action the policeman could take. No laws were broken, no peace disturbed, and nobody seemed in danger. It was as yet an unspoken observation.

There was little understanding of mental health. There were the sane in society and the mad in the asylums, and those in between were merely passing from one to the other. There was no real concept or training on the power of conversation.

During that summer of change in 1905, Peter wrote to his Prudential Supervisor, Mr Edwin Henry James Read, to let him know that he had used some of the company's money for his own purposes, something he should not do. He asked Mr Read to come to Amesbury to investigate him.

Edwin Read was a year younger than Peter, but Peter was, of course, no stranger to younger men being his professional senior, and Read, ironically, was no stranger to the anguish of financial worry and poor books. Some years earlier he had run several greengrocer businesses in and around Portsmouth, and in 1889 his own business became insolvent, with the judge largely blaming Read's lack of record-keeping. Read later went on to start working as a salesman for the Prudential, overcame his aversion to book-keeping and progressed to be a District Superintendent.

Read was concerned at what he would find. He had encountered pilfering before, but never anyone reporting themselves to him. He took the earliest train to Amesbury and visited the Heads in their Earls Court Road cottage.

Sitting down, he examined Peter's books. "*Not only are your books in good order, Mr Head, we, the company, owe* you *the sum of £4.*"

"*Oh*," Peter replied, and said nothing further of the matter he had reported. Mr Read felt an incipient concern for Peter's mental health, but nothing was to be done. Had Read thought it wise to speak to Sgt Scott, maybe that added piece of information may have caused the policeman to do something more and could have stopped the course of events that were about to unfold.

CHAPTER 14

The Tragedy –
'I shall some day lose my reasoning'

In the week beginning Monday, 18th September, 1905, Peter travelled to London to visit his ailing mother, who was by now completely unable to earn a living as a dressmaker. She was often confined to bed with bedsores developing, and was receiving the most minimal care. This may well have been an expensive visit.

He felt increasingly affected by the turmoil life had thrown at him, and the wrestling he was having within his own mind was amplifying all his problems beyond their reality. His nest egg was gone, lost in the sand and sheds of his failed chicken farm. He was no longer applauded and cheered while singing his funny songs and doing his comic turns. He had been a respected instructor of arms and drill and discipline, but what was he now? Just someone selling promises in the event of doom. Plus, half of the people who said yes to an insurance policy failed to show up at the doctor's appointment. Where was their discipline? People always let him down.

What little money he had was being thrown into the pot of the Marylebone Infirmary, feeding and housing his wife and seven children, and sending money for his eldest daughter. He did not resent paying his mother's bills, but then, what had she done for him? He had been only twelve years old when he was sent away from his home to live with no parental love in the care of the choristers and clergy of St Peter's Church.

What would become of his children if he went bankrupt? What would people say? He could barely pay to keep them all clothed and fed as it was. His cards appeared to him to have been suddenly dealt so cruelly. There was little fairness in this world, and what had he done, having so many children who had to make their way in such a bleak and callous existence? And Florence, what of her? Yes, what of Florence? His head hurt. He felt very unwell.

The reality, had he the clarity of mind to see it, or someone who could talk to him and tell him, was different. Yes, he had lost his savings, but there was still a little money tied up in the land for future realisation. He would always receive his military pension, and he was doing well selling his insurance. The burden brought about by his mother would sadly not be for too long, and Amy was growing up and would be working herself soon. Looking from the outside, life did not appear to be as bad as for many others who scrimped, scraped and starved during these times. There were those far less fortunate both inside and outside of the Amesbury workhouse.

On that Wednesday evening, he took the train from London back to Amesbury and ruminated deeply about his perceived woes. From the railway station he went straight to the 28th Brigade mess in Bulford. He spoke briefly to his great friend, Sergeant Major Stamp. During this conversation, Peter appeared to be his usual self, but later that evening, after Stamp had retired to his quarters, Peter complained to the caterer that he was suffering from a severe cold and experiencing pains in his head.

Later that night, he returned home and complained to Florence about the pains in his head, saying, "*I shall some day lose my reasoning.*"

On the Thursday evening, Peter met a prospective insurance client whom he took to meet Dr Lockyer for examination. He was still thinking about new policies, even with other plans invading his mind. He was a disciplined and proud man and he would not fail to attend a meeting he had already arranged. He would not be a disappointment to others as so many others were to him.

Stamp saw Peter Head in the mess again on the Thursday night, but didn't have the opportunity to speak with him. It may have been that Peter avoided him on purpose. He had made decisions and did not want to give himself away. Earlier that day, as he waited for the children to come home from school, he had written to his friend to explain what he was to do, and he may well have had the letter in his pocket. He had already decided that it was the last time his children would return home from school.

On the morning of Friday, 22nd September, 1905, the children went to school for the last time. Baby Frederick stayed with Florence. Several days later, Richard Wilson would bring Florence back to this moment. She mentions no arguments, no disharmony in the family. No one can say with certainty that this was the case. What happens within the four walls of an Englishman's castle cannot be known outside of it. On this day, Florence was feeling unwell.

So was Peter. His head was racing, pounding, and he was resolute. He had made his mind up and written one letter. He could see nothing to change his mind. The world was not a good place. He feared for the future, his and his children's. He did not want his children to live a life of disappointment. The world had nothing to offer them. The world let everyone down. Everything now worried him.

It was a dreary, grey, damp autumn day. Peter sat down with some writing paper and a pen and wrote another two letters. One of those was to Mr Read, the Prudential Superintendent.

'... by the time you receive this I shall be no more. I am worried by the wretched state of my books and by domestic troubles.'

He walked around the village of Amesbury, his mind in a furious muddle of resigned fate. From Earls Court Road he walked past the school to the High Street. He stopped at Mrs Witt's barber's shop in Salisbury Street, where he bought a new razor. A clean, sharp edge. Sharper, perhaps, than the other one he had in his pocket.

He walked to the church. Neither Peter nor his children would have ever heard the bells peal from the church tower of the Abbey Church of St Mary and St Melor. During the incumbency of Rev Reginald Fawkes, great efforts had been made to make necessary restorations in the church, particularly to enable the tower to accommodate the bells again safely. Fawkes had worked tirelessly to that aim, as well as raising funds and contributing himself to build a reading room and Men's Club.

Rev Fawkes was not in the church when Peter visited, and I wonder how matters may have progressed had he been there. Peter signed into the church visitors' book and told his God what he was about to do. He was concerned for his soul, but found little solace or reason to cause him to change his mind.

He had written a letter for Rev Fawkes.

'Reverend Sir,

I beg to thank you for your kindness to me. I am sorry I have lost all hope of getting on. I am completely worn out with worry and reverses. God forgive me for all

*but I have tried so hard to be a good man and to lead
a good life. Don't think too hard of me. I have just
been to your church and asked my God to forgive me
and have mercy on me.*

Bury us all in the same grave.

Your obedient servant

Peter R Head'

Although he had decided what must happen, he did not
want to be parted from the children, and told Fawkes so.

He walked towards the post office, which necessitated
passing the police station. With his head down, he made no
eye contact with Sergeant Scott, who was outside talking to
some builders as Peter walked past. Sergeant Scott watched
the usually gregarious man he knew well pass him without
giving him the time of day, and commented to the workmen,
"He is going out of his mind fast."

It was an ominous observation, and in terms of timing
he had never been more correct in a character assessment,
but as is the dilemma many police officers experience, you
often cannot do anything about things that are not yet done.
Many an officer will know individuals who they think will kill
one day, but they can do nothing because those individuals
have done nothing yet. It is an impossible situation to be
in control of, other than enacting a blind hope that if you
engage a person in such apparent turmoil with conversation,
it may help.

Peter went to the post office, where he sent off a small
package and letter to Stamp and a letter to Read. Possibly,
the letter to Rev Fawkes was also posted, though Peter may
have left it in the church. There was no turning back now. He
was committed. Letters saying what he would do had been

sent, an irreversible countdown had started. He put the pencil and some paper in his pocket and walked towards home.

Peter returned to their cottage in Earls Court Road, where Florence was asleep on the bed with baby Freddie. She was still feeling out of sorts and Peter quietly made her a cup of tea, before gently waking her to drink it.

"I am going to take the baby out. Will you dress him? I might show him to Mrs Ford," Peter said to the groggy Florence.

"But it's damp outside, Peter, is it not better to leave him here?" she replied.

"I am proud of him and want to show him off. Are you not proud?" came his fatherly reply.

Florence acquiesced and dressed the baby for him. Peter took Freddie in his arms and bade her goodbye. It was the last time Florence would see her husband and her son. There was no sign of what would occur in the coming hours. It would be a few minutes that she would relive to herself many times over.

They had no pram, so Peter carried the baby in his arms down Earls Court Road and turned right to the school, where he knocked on the door. It was answered by the headmaster himself, Charles Hallett. The two men shook hands and Hallett jokingly asked if Peter had a new occupation as a nurse, to which Peter laughed and replied, saying, "Yes." The baby was happy and smiling at the teacher.

Patting the baby on the face, Mr Hallett said, "He looks strong and well."

Peter replied, "Yes, he's a happy chap. Doesn't he look strong and healthy. He looks a picture of health. I wonder if Mildred might be allowed to leave school now and come with me?"

Mr Hallett agreed and went to tell her. Mildred Grace Head then left at the girls' entrance of the school, but Peter was waiting at the boys' entrance. He waited a while, then returned to the door, which this time was answered by Mrs Hallett, who told him that Mildred had left. Mildred eventually found her father and they waited at the boys' entrance for her brothers to emerge. This brief confusion concerning Mildred later resulted in a number of conflicting versions of events in the papers. Young Florence Ellen had been briefly detained by a teacher, and Peter sent one of the others in for her. Florence eventually came out, and the two girls, three lads and baby boy left with their father.

Some newspapers would confuse Elsie (Monkey) with Mildred. At first, they explained that Elsie was missed because of leaving via the female entrance, when, in fact, as Mr Hallett explained when asked, that was Mildred. Later that week, a report stated Elsie had left school earlier to do some shopping for her mother. Many years later, in 1962, a fellow classmate reportedly told a local newspaper that Elsie had, in fact, been held in class and wasn't allowed to leave early. After school, she had been sent on a shopping errand by Florence and then not allowed to join her father and siblings because of the time. It is difficult to know exactly what happened, but it is likely that Monkey was held back. Mildred must have had a later finishing time that day, hence Peter asking for her and not just waiting like he did for the others. This is further suggested by the fact that when Hallett allowed her to leave, he cancelled her attendance record for the day. However it played out, Peter gathered all his children except Elsie. He had no time to try and find her and was conscious of what needed to be done, and when.

Peter now had six of his eight children. He did not take them home. He told them they were going to have some fun and play games on the field, and despite the damp, grey day, they walked in the direction of Salisbury, with the eldest, Mildred Grace, proudly carrying her baby brother.

At 1630 hours, Henry Bryant, a farm labourer, was walking home down South Mill Hill towards Amesbury town when he met Peter and the children. Peter was holding hands with the youngest walker, Alfred. Henry Bryant did not know Peter, but they passed the time of day as they walked in opposite directions, and Bryant saw that Mildred was carrying baby Freddie in the procession of her siblings, Florence, Peter, William and Alfred.

Henry Bryant was the last person to see them all alive. What a shock he was to have the next day when he heard the news describing a scene so incongruous to the one he had witnessed.

Peter had made up his mind about what needed to happen. He had prepared and posted and left his letters. He knew that when he moved, he had to be quick; he could not be caught midway through. He could not be stopped. It was all too late. Peter was already a man who had hanged himself from a tree, and even if he changed his mind, all the twigs and branches he might reach out for to save him would break in his grasp.

Their walk along Salisbury Street and into South Mill Hill was joyous. Though missing the second eldest of their little tribe, the children skipped and played along the way, teasing each other and carrying the baby. Peter was outwardly disguising the monumental mental anguish he was feeling and holding back the tsunami of violence he knew he had decided to mete out.

As they walked along the tree-lined avenue towards the field they had played in so many times before, they played as children play. Laughing and running around and feeling the joy of having so many siblings to play with and a father who joked and played, who ran around with them and who took so much pleasure from their existence. They loved their father. Their brave dad, who all the soldiers in Scotland had called 'Sir' and who was so self-assured, so strong. Who always thought of them first.

The two elder boys held hands with little Alfred, three months shy of his third birthday, and together with Mildred, who had handed over the baby to her younger sister, Florence, raced ahead into the field. The field had recently been harvested and hayricks were dotted around it like tepees.

Past a hayrick they skipped as the land curved slightly up and away. Peter was behind his children as seven-year-old Florence had fallen to her knees carrying Freddie. Peter was in anguish, thoughts racing around his head like an uncoordinated murmuration of starlings, bouncing and colliding with each other and not seeing any way out. He could not keep hold of any rational thought other than that which he must do. He had to do it. He had told the vicar. He had told Stamp. He had told Read. He had told God. He had to. He was no coward. He had to do it now, and he had to do it quickly.

With the baby on the floor and the rick between them and the other children, he comforted little Florence and brushed her down. Taking his cut-throat razor from his pocket, he turned her around to face away from him, and then in an instant he cut her throat from ear to ear, nearly decapitating her. It was quick and the noise of the flow of blood pushed out from the last beats of a racing heart and the brief bubbling from her filling lungs was lost in the wind. He lay her down under the rick. The baby next, with less haste and more deliberation to ensure the severance of the jugular. He only needed to cut halfway across the tiny throat.

67

Dropping the bloodied razor, he lay down the limp, lifeless body of Freddie, his youngest son, only nine months old, and walked quickly towards his other children. He shouted to William, Peter and Mildred to hide quickly, telling them that he and little Alfred would seek them out. He pulled out his handkerchief and, as the others ran, he blindfolded Alfred. He could not risk the older ones seeing anything before he could reach them, in case they ran and screamed, and he did not want to risk the toddler seeing anything anyway. He told the little blindfolded Alfred to stay still and count loudly, and then, having watched where each of the other three had concealed themselves, he approached them quickly, one at a time, out of sight of each other, using the different hayricks for cover. Reassuring them with the loving hands that they trusted so implicitly, he took out the fresh, sharp razor and in turn swung each trusting child around, and with a deft, deliberate motion drew his blade hard across their throats. To the bone. The still-counting Alfred heard his father's approach and his comforting voice, before feeling those familiar large hands on his shoulders. Then his throat was cut, too, and the life blood projected out from his body.

The deed was done. Peter Head had crossed the very line that Sergeant Major Stamp would read of the following morning – and more.

He was not yet finished, though. He gathered the bodies of William, Peter and Alfred and lined them up like a macabre parade. The three bodies lay like little soldiers. He removed his own jacket and waistcoat and folded them up on the ground. He unbuttoned his shirt. He then took his pencil and one last piece of writing paper. He knew there would be an inquest. He wanted one last say. Perhaps he thought about writing to his wife, but instead he addressed the note to the coroner. He folded the letter up and put it inside his bowler hat, which he placed upon his pile of outer clothing. Surveying the scene of his poor dead, mutilated children, the grief and realisation of what he had done and of what was coming next hit him like a train. He was a murderer. His poor children. But he was no coward. If he stayed there, at a later date he would hang by the neck till dead. Being caught alive was never part of the plan. He rolled back his shirt and held out the bloodied but still sharp new razor. He took one more look at the world, at the bloodied stubble of the hay, and at the boys next to him, exposing the inside of their throats, no less than stuck piglets. Then he sighed with that final resignation unique only to those knowing they are about to die (or those who have witnessed that) and with determination and brutal force he pushed the sharp razor deeply across his own throat from ear to ear, severing every sinew of skin, flesh, vein and artery in its gristly path. With wild, shocked, open eyes, he fell back, the momentary pain disappearing with his consciousness as the oxygen flow to his brain stopped, and the razor slipped from his lifeless grip.

The order of the deaths as I have just presented it is conjecture on my part, having considered at length the scene described by PC Wells and Sergeant Scott. The opinion of those visiting the scene was that Florence had run away with the baby, having seen her father kill the others and realising what was coming for her next, and that he had chased them before committing the deed, causing her to fall and graze her knees as he caught her. This contemporary opinion was based purely on the fact that Florence and Freddie were nearest the field entrance. I believe that Peter, despite being about to commit the most horrific crime against his children, would still have wanted them to experience the least amount of stress. If she was holding Freddie, it would be natural for Florence to be lagging behind the others, and having a hayrick and lie of the land for cover, it seems credible that Peter would have acted in the chronological order I have described.

The one piece of evidence which is for the argument that Florence and Freddie were last was the fact that one of the razors was by the side of the baby and one was by Peter himself. It is feasible that he killed all the children with one blade, leaving it with the baby as the last victim, then used the brand-new sharp razor on himself.

I prefer my version. Peter would have been quick, decisive. It was a military strike. He could not have any of them escape or make a noise that would alert anybody passing by. Also, the severing of the windpipe with the jugular would prevent any screams. It is, of course, preferable to think that none of the children saw it coming.

He was now the biggest mass killer the county of Wiltshire had known, but Peter was no coward. He told everyone that.

CHAPTER 15

The Gruesome Discovery

Elsie Mabel, the mischievous Monkey, was home with her mother. Florence did not know where the rest of her children or her husband were, and as the evening became night she began to increasingly fret.

"Where on God's Earth could they be?"

At about 11pm, Florence left the cottage and walked into town, where she found PC Wells standing in the square in Salisbury Street. He could see she was worried.

"Can I speak to you, Constable?" asked the anxious Mrs Head in her soft Worcestershire accent.

"Yes, ma'am," replied the young officer in his broad Wiltshire one.

They walked a little way down the road and stood near the bank. "Have you seen my husband and children today?" asked Florence.

"I have not," said the police officer.

"My husband went away at three thirty this afternoon with the baby and said he was going to take him down to show someone in the village. He said he would be back at tea time. I have also heard since that he fetched the five children from school, and I think it is strange that he has not returned, as it is getting late." PC Wells noted down what she said, and then she added, "I will go back home and see if he has come now."

PC Wells followed her home, remembering from his training that most missing people are found in the place from where they were reported missing. There was, of course, no sign of their return, so he went back to the police station to report the matter to Sergeant Scott. Sergeant Scott was older, more experienced, and therefore a little harder and more resilient.

Following instructions from Sergeant Scott, PC Wells set off along the road out of town towards Salisbury. He searched a little way, and on coming back, turned up South Mill Hill, following the track away from the road to the fields. It was dark and rainy and there was no street lighting. Aided only by his hand-held 'bullseye' lamp and a weak moon fighting through the cloudy, damp sky, he walked a small way into the first field.

He tentatively walked twenty yards or so and came across the first hayrick. Suddenly, in the eerie light his lamp gave off and with great shock, young Wells saw two small bodies. He had found little Florence Ellen and the baby Freddie. They were lying completely still; Florence with a gaping opening right across her throat, and the baby with a deep cut across half of his. Blood was spattered across the hay stubble. Bending down to touch them, with his heart in his mouth, he found they were both cold and stiff.

A uniform does not prevent its wearer experiencing alarm or fear, yet the sense of duty it can instil can help them get through that kind of trauma. At the time.

Shocked, PC Wells shone his lamp around and, seeing nothing else immediately in the vicinity, he needed no encouragement to leave the field and report the find directly to Sergeant Scott. As he walked along the dark lane leading back towards the main road, no doubt in the back of his mind he was playing out the scenario of a crazed knife-wielding ghoul coming out from the trees and inflicting him with the same gruesome wound. Acutely aware of every sound of the wind in the trees and every unidentified animal howl, he hurried from the scene of the crime with his own heart beating hard from the exertion and shock of the discovery.

The main road was some two hundred and seventy yards from the bodies, and the sight of it gave some relief, if only a little, to PC Wells as he quick-marched back to the station, arriving there at midnight.

Sergeant Scott listened to his story. Quickly, he gathered his coat and lamp and they both left the station. The preservation of life and property is the primary aim of the police, and several possible different scenarios were filling Scott's mind. To cover the possibility that they would find injured children, too, and also to start gathering any evidence from the dead, they called on Dr Lockyer on the way and together all three walked to the deposition site found by Wells.

As the dimly gas-lit roads gave way to darker paths, Sergeant Scott gathered his thoughts. Had Peter Head killed his children? Should he have said something to him earlier that day when he had seen him? Maybe Head is waiting to be arrested or gone on the run with his other children. He didn't want anything to go wrong with this case, were he to catch a murderer. Only two years earlier, Sergeant Scott had arrested a woman called Harriet Wilds for murdering her newly born baby at Bulford. He was more than sure about where the guilt lay, but the officers who attended the initial scene had not approached with an open mind of suspicion, and consequently the scene was not searched properly, and the murder weapon was not found. The evidence of the doctor's opinion was insufficient to expel reasonable doubt from the minds of the jury and, in Scott's opinion, a guilty woman was let off the hook. He had learnt the lesson of the importance of disciplined scene management, and it was not going to happen again. This scene would be searched thoroughly and everything seized.

The cold, stiff bodies of Florence and Freddie were quickly located. Sergeant Scott took possession of the blood-stained razor found next to Freddie, and Dr Lockyer confirmed life extinct. There was no doubt in Scott's mind that this time he had the weapon concerned. This could be the exhibit to convict the murderer. Dr Lockyer noted the grazing to Florence's knees.

They walked a further sixty yards into the field where, under another hayrick, they found ten-year-old Mildred Grace Head lying on her back, a huge, open, bloody wound across her throat evident to all. A further twenty-two yards into the field, the three boys, William Robert, Peter and Alfred, were lined up next to each other under a hayrick. All had deep cuts across their throats, and Alfred, the youngest there, had a handkerchief fashioned as a blindfold tied across his open eyes. Three little boy soldiers.

Lying next to them was the former Sergeant Major, recognised by all those there, even in the dim lamplight. The officer on parade, as if taking the salute and inspecting his little men, was lying on his back with a razor just by his hand on the ground. His shirt collar was unbuttoned and rolled back and a deep cavity across his neck stretched from ear to ear. The stain of his expelled blood had sprayed across the wet stubble. So confident and hard was the strike, and so sharp was the blade, that in the swipe across his windpipe it had been completely severed. Death had come so quickly that his eyes remained open and wild, staring into eternity.

Sergeant Scott took possession of the second razor. He knew now that there would be no murder conviction, but that he must still gather all the evidence available. Five yards from Peter's body lay the neat pile consisting of his jacket, waistcoat, collar and tie. A neat pile like a uniform folded on a barrack-room bed. On top of that was his distinctive bowler hat. The fashion of the Prudential man and his uniform in civil life, but there was nothing civil about this. Tucked into Head's hat, Sergeant Scott found a note hastily written in pencil and addressed to the coroner. Peter had known the process.

'All are dead and in heaven. God have mercy on my soul. I have been a terrible sufferer.'

Dr Lockyer examined and noted the condition of the bodies and the police officers arranged for a horse and cart. The bodies were all reverently loaded upon the cart and taken to the mortuary at the Workhouse not far away.

Sergeant Scott then made the walk that most police officers experience several times in their careers and never forget doing. The walk that takes them to the point of someone else's life that is about to change forever. During the walk, the person who they are visiting sits in hope, and within moments of the officer's arrival, all prospect of hope is extinguished forever, and that officer is eternally associated with the death of their loved ones.

Scott walked to the cottage in Earls Court Road, where Florence sat awake, cold and scared. Monkey was dozing lightly in her bed, wondering where her siblings were. The scream and sobs of her mother would bring that wondering to an end.

Sergeant Scott was late going off duty that night. He spent what time he thought proper with Florence, then left her to her grief and returned to the station to write up a report of what had taken place. He then sent a request for the coroner to attend in the morning and sent a despatch to inform

Superintendent Longstone of Wiltshire Police and a request to Portsmouth Police to inform Florence's brother, Albert, of the deaths and ask him to attend. The bodies required formal identification and he knew that he could not impose that gruesome task upon Florence.

Peter Robert Head in Royal Artillery uniform wearing the
Egyptian Medal with Tel-El-Kebir Clasp, and
The Khedive's Star. *c*1883.
Courtesy of Cotterell Family

Amy Matilda Head *c*1887
Courtesy of Liz Mathias and Gill Davies

Amesbury National School *c* early 1900s, from where
Peter Head collected five of the children.

Courtesy of Jim Fuller

> 264
> 1905
>
> Class IV: Lesson on "The Railway"
>
> Sep: 22 Mr. Head called and asked if Mildred
> may leave the school – 3.40. She was
> allowed to go – Her attendance has
> been cancelled.
>
> 25 Mildred Head + Florence Head are
> dead –

Mr Hallett's entry in the school log for
September 22nd and 25th 1905.

Courtesy of Wiltshire and Swindon History Centre F8/500/6/1/2

Joan and Ben and spaniel on the SS Rotterdam on their way
back from the USA. August 1960

Courtesy of Cotterell family

Monkey and Peter Cotterell early 1980s in the gardens of the
Château de Versailles.

Courtesy of Cotterell family

Peter Cotterell laying flowers at the grave of the Head children.
2005

Courtesy of Cotterell family

The gravestone placed by Rex Reynolds many years after the
murders commemorating the children and marking the spot of
their and their father's burial. Amesbury cemetery 2023.

Photograph by Neil Berrett

CHAPTER 16

Immediate Aftermath and the Jury

A cross the weekend, the bodies lay in the mortuary of the Workhouse in Amesbury.

At about 9am the following morning, Saturday, 22nd September, Sergeant Major Stamp went into the Guard Room, where there was mail waiting for him. He noticed that the letter and the small parcel had the same handwriting. He opened them carefully and then immediately travelled to Amesbury. It is clear that the letter had been written on the Thursday.

'My Dear Stamp

I'm going to cross the line with my four boys. All hope of successful work gone so I am resolved to take my life and the four boys as well for I cannot leave the little chaps. Will you accept my medals as I have no one else to leave them to. With Many thanks to you and your friends in the 28th battery I say goodbye.

Yours (not a coward)

PR Head.

Ps. The youngsters are coming home from school, how little they think it will be their last return home.'

The package Stamp received contained Peter's three medals: the Egyptian Medal, Khedive's Star and Long Service Medal. Strange that he felt that he could not leave them for Florence or Amy, and clear that he had not expected Monkey to survive when he wrote the letter.

The coroner received the message. Richard Wilson had had a busy week, but once again duty called, and he travelled to Amesbury from his Salisbury home. He met with Doctor Lockyer and Sergeant Scott. Superintendent Longstone also came into Amesbury. This would be a high-profile case with a lot of press interest.

Mr Wilson had two initial jobs to do. Firstly, visit the widow, and secondly, arrange for a jury to be assembled for the inquest to be held on the coming Monday. It was a clear case and there was no need for it to be hanging around. He would spend the weekend going through the investigation and clear it up with an inquest on Monday.

The twelve men of the jury were selected very locally, and most were probably known to the socially active Richard Wilson. Most would have known the Head family and certainly knew each other. Two of these men had very recently experienced the pain of burying one of their own children.

Henry Macey Gane was to be the foreman of the jury. He was a fifty-four-year-old who had lived for many years in Salisbury Street, Amesbury, first making his way as a skilled blacksmith like his father and then becoming the only slightly less laborious coal merchant. Henry was joined on the bench by the following men:

Edmund James Brown, a fifty-one-year-old music teacher who had grown up in Salisbury Street before moving to Earls Court Road, near to Peter and Florence Head. He is the 'Mr Brown' referred to occasionally in the newspapers at the time as the organist for the St Mary and St Melor Church, Amesbury.

Christopher Grace, a thirty-six-year-old gardener, also living in Salisbury Street, who coincidentally had a daughter called Mildred Grace.

John Soul was, at thirty-seven, running his bakery, grocery and general store in Salisbury Street, Amesbury.

John Barnes, forty-four years old, had been the landlord of the Greyhound Inn, Amesbury, which was situated close to where the Heads lived.

John Shepherd was a sixty-nine-year-old farm labourer who more recently was an engine driver on a farm. He lived a little further out of Amesbury towards Salisbury, in Stratford-sub-Castle.

John George Mugford was a Devonian and was the landlord of the King's Arms in Amesbury.

Bertram Hale was a thirty-five-year-old man running an outfitters' shop in the High Street, Amesbury. He had been a Petty Officer on the SS *Britannia*. Having served seventeen years in the Royal Navy, he moved to Amesbury in 1901 to become assistant church warden.

William Frederick Corp, a thirty-five-year-old former commercial traveller, had taken the licence of the New Inn, Amesbury, the week before the murders.

Francis Everett also once had a pub, the White Hart, in Longham, Dorset, but had settled into butchery as a trade. He moved to Amesbury in the 1890s and, being the only butcher in Salisbury Street, he would have known Peter, Florence and the children. Francis had only recently buried his own twenty-two-year-old daughter, Mary Harriet Everett, who appears in the burial register just before Peter Head. Francis was the oldest juror.

Frederick W. Underwood was a thirty-year-old plumber and decorator who a little later lived in Church Street.

Jesse Medlam was a forty-five-year-old estate manager, living with his wife and children in the High Street, Amesbury, next door to the Underwoods. He was a man with sons of a similar age to the Head boys who, no doubt, knew the family.

Having had the jury selected, coroner Richard Wilson visited Florence. With Monkey there, too, the only surviving full sibling of seven trying to make some sense out of it all in her young mind, it was a difficult visit. It was quickly clear to Wilson that Florence would be unable to attend, let alone give evidence at, the inquest, and he took a statement from her there and then. In between the waves of realisation, the immense fatigue of worry, followed by a grief-stricken sleepless night, she was only able to give him a brief outline of her marriage and Peter's outlook.

Wilson was used to dealing with people at the apotheosis of their grief. He was more than accustomed to dealing with child deaths and suicide, but not on this scale. He was a kind, thoughtful and empathetic man, but a pragmatic lawyer, too, and any information that would educate his decision-making was important. It was cases like this that emphasised to him how correct it was to have won that old argument as to whether the coroner should be a law man or a medical man.

Florence Head spoke about her life. She was now thirty-four years old. She had given birth to seven healthy children and followed her husband around the country. Now six were dead and so was he. Wilson noted down aspects of what she told him.

'I have been married nearly 12 years. My husband left the Army about three years ago. He was a sergeant major in the Royal Garrison Artillery. We have been in Amesbury nearly 2 years, and previous to that we had a poultry farm in Andover, but we had not sufficient capital to make it a success. He never threatened to take his life, and when he read of any cases of suicide in the papers he would say, "He must've been a coward.

If anything happened to me I would face the music."
We lived happily together. About eight years ago he
had a fall off the ramparts at Portsmouth and he was
laid up. I think it affected his head. On Friday not
feeling well, I lay down on my bed with the baby and
fell asleep. My husband woke me at three o'clock,
bringing me a cup of tea which he had made me. He
then asked me to dress the baby, that he might take
him to show Mrs Ford. I advised him not to take the
baby as it was damp. And he said he was proud of the
baby, and asked me if I was not also. My husband's
pension was nearly 20 shillings a week. He complained
of pains in his head when he came home from London
on Wednesday night and he said then, "I shall some
day lose my reasoning." His first thoughts were always
for me and the children.'

It is likely that Florence's statement to Richard Wilson
was a little more comprehensive than this, but this was all
the newspapers reported.

Peter Head had left letters to his friend Stamp, his manager
Read and his vicar, Rev Fawkes. He had also left a note by his
own body after committing the awful acts. No explanation
to Florence. There was no letter left for his wife who, he
must have known, was about to face the most unbearable
emotional trauma one can think of. Perhaps she did have a
letter, but the contents were not something she wanted to
share.

Florence had certainly not shared everything with the
coroner or the police. She had neglected, or purposefully
left out, one huge pertinent fact. She was pregnant. No one
knew. She was only about five or six weeks pregnant. This
was her eighth pregnancy and she may well have known all
the signs and suspected by then. It is likely that was why

she had felt unwell that fateful day and needed sleep in the afternoon. The question as to whether Peter knew this fact is a very difficult one to answer. How would he have taken such news? Was it the catalyst that threw his mental state over the edge? Another mouth to feed at a time when he thought that he was already in dire financial ruin? Was this the 'domestic trouble' that he had referred to in the letter to Read? Really, only conjecture can answer these remaining questions. It is also quite possible that not even Florence was aware of her state that week and that Peter did not know.

There are many recorded cases that where a man commits such a despicable crime as this, he is 'getting back' at the mother for some perceived wrong, as part of an escalating ongoing violent domestic dispute. All the evidence available here points away from that being the case. The only exception is that mention of 'domestic troubles' written in the letter to Read. Florence spoke only of a good life together and Peter's kindness. Neighbours spoke of his fondness of the children, and there were no suggestions or contemporary mentions of any domestic strife between Florence and Peter. Many years later, in 1962, a newspaper report recalling the incident printed a view from an old school mate of the Head children reporting that it was said that Peter had done it because of rumours that Florence was seeing too much of an 'insurance man'. This seems to be a case of rumours changing along the passage of time and speculation. Peter *was* the insurance man. The report contains a number of other provable inaccuracies, so I would not want this book to be a continuance of such an argument. Florence was pregnant with Peter's child, of that there becomes no doubt, and she always spoke of him, then and after, in endearing terms, as did both Elsie and Amy.

It was those very questions that Florence sought to avoid by choosing not to mention her new pregnancy, if she knew about it. Considering everything available both then and now, it does seem that mentioning the pregnancy at the time would not have changed any outcome, but whether it actually was a catalyst to making Peter take the decisions he did would only ever have been known to him and possibly her. Throughout the writing and researching of this, however, I have come to the view that Peter did not know of the pregnancy and that up to that week, as Florence said to Wilson, their marriage was happy and close.

It is true also that Peter did not mention his wife or his daughters in any of the correspondence he left. He only refers to taking his 'four boys' with him. He also sent his medals to Stamp knowing that his wife and oldest daughter at least would survive. If his initial intention had been only to kill the boys, he would not have first asked for Mildred at the school. Perhaps the patriarchal mindset he, the military and society in general was in at that time, made him feel it was only necessary to talk about the boys. The apparent complete lack of consideration for Florence is inexplicable. Considering the times, however, it is not indicative of a poor relationship between the two, either.

CHAPTER 17

The Inquest

Superintendent Longstone of Wiltshire Police had come to Amesbury to oversee their part of the investigation and give Sergeant Scott what help he needed for the inquest. In that year of 1905, murder would rank jointly with pneumonia as the third biggest killer in Amesbury, and Peter Head was responsible for all of them. This was the biggest mass murder the county had seen, and, in fact, I believe it remains so. It was, though, very much a clear-cut case. Even those with the broadest of minds could see that in contrast with the infamous Rode House child murder of 1864, there was no requirement for any detectives to come from London to investigate.

Superintendent Longstone was also someone familiar with child murder, cruelty and suicide. A long-serving officer, he had seen his share of tragedy and suffering. Only four years earlier, he had been involved in the investigation of a very high-profile and surprising case of child cruelty. The defendant was Annie Elizabeth Penruddocke, wife of Charles Penruddocke, a Justice of the Peace who lived at the family seat of Compton Park, Compton Chamberlayne, near Wilton, Wiltshire. Superintendent Longstone had executed a warrant at the house and, finding one of the five children to be bruised and malnourished, took her into care and launched an investigation. The child had been singled out among her siblings by the mother and treated extremely harshly, including being made to stand on one leg for hours and to run outside in the cold, as well as having nettles rubbed on her, being beaten and refused food. There were social challenges in taking the prosecution forward and it ended up being tried in the Old Bailey, where a successful prosecution took place, albeit with a paltry sentence. The child lived to her nineties, whereas two of her brothers who were treated well by their mother were killed in the First World War and the other later killed himself. Despite being a Superintendent, Longstone had shown himself to be no 'establishment man', determined that the case and justice should prevail.

The twelve men of the Heads' inquest jury convened at 5pm that Monday in the boardroom of Amesbury Workhouse. After Richard Wilson swore them in, their first task was to go to the mortuary and view the bodies, something a jury of an inquest was compelled to do at the time. Not a pleasant task to see any dead body, viewing the bodies of six children so brutally slaughtered was a traumatic thing. The matron and nurse of the workhouse did their best to make the experience as painless as possible and dressed the bodies in the best way they could. In fact, the matron did such a good job in protecting the jury from the complete horror that one of the jurors later wrote an open letter to the newspaper thanking the workhouse for those efforts. They all then took the short walk to South Mill Hill to examine the scene, where Sergeant Scott no doubt showed the jury, Coroner, and Superintendent the locations where the bodies they had just seen had met their deaths. The rain had only slightly diluted the stained hay stubble, which still gave away the violence of the events of three evenings earlier. It was a solemn visit.

Back at the workhouse boardroom, Richard Wilson, the diligent Coroner, commenced proceedings. He made a brief introduction, during which he expressed his belief that very little evidence would be brought before them regarding the deaths, describing the incident as a tragedy which he thought could hardly be paralleled in this country. In fact, it had been a while, but in London in 1854 there had been a similar murder of six children by a former nursemaid of Queen Victoria called Mary Ann Brough. She, incidentally, had also complained of head pains and had also used the phrase, 'One day I shall lose my reasoning.' In 1860, when Peter Head was barely two years old, there had been a strikingly similar incident where William Henry Whitworth, a Sergeant in the Royal Artillery stationed in Sandown on the Isle of Wight, had cut the throats of his six children and his wife, killing them all. He made no attempt on his own life.

Wilson's opening statements almost directed what verdict the jury should find from the outset, when he said that he believed there would be no difficulty in arriving at the conclusion that the six poor children were murdered by their father, who afterwards cut his own throat. He did, however, reserve an opinion over criminal responsibility until the close of the inquiry. He also informed those present that the mother would not be able to attend and that there should be no objection to this or delay in the inquest waiting for her attendance.

Albert Edward King arrived in Amesbury later on the Saturday or Sunday. He was Florence Head's brother from Portsmouth and currently had care of Peter's eldest daughter, Amy, even though he was not actually related to her. Amy was now seventeen and probably already working.

On the Monday, Albert King had the distressing task of viewing the bodies of his nieces, nephews and brother-in-law, in order to provide evidence of official identification. It is difficult to say how well he knew the children to actually identify them, as he had not seen Peter for two years and may therefore never have met the younger children. However, it is probable that Florence had taken a trip to Portsmouth more recently. We know that earlier in 1905 she had returned to Andover and perhaps she went from there. That said, there was, of course, no disputing the identification, and Sergeant Scott himself could have done so.

Albert was the first person called to take the witness stand, and he gave his evidence of identification as well as a little background on his brother-in-law. When asked about the ages of the surviving daughters, Albert said that Amy, from the first marriage, was seventeen years old and lived with him, and that Elsie Mabel was twelve. Sergeant Scott interjected and corrected this latter statement, as Monkey was, in fact, only nine.

Sergeant Scott then took the oath and gave the coroner and jury a detailed account of the steps he took after being notified by PC Wells of Mrs Head's report of the missing family. With stoic confidence, he described the scene with which he had been confronted in the field, dark as it was. He was no stranger to a courtroom and had given evidence before Mr Wilson several times, most recently with the Bulford child death for which he had arrested the mother and not found a weapon. Longstone was the senior police officer here, but Scott knew this town and its people. He knew Peter Robert Head.

Dr Lockyer was next up and corroborated the Sergeant's evidence, having been with him on the night. He told the coroner and jury of the extent of the injuries and hypothesised as to the time of death. He also told of having seen Peter the evening before with an 'insurance man', meaning, on this occasion, a client, and explained how worried Peter would seem on those occasions when he had completed the paperwork for a prospective client who subsequently failed to turn up to see the doctor. When asked, the doctor assessed Peter as seeming to him perfectly sane and sober at that time.

Charles Hallett, the headmaster of Amesbury School, was sworn in and gave his evidence. He spoke of Head attending the school at 3.40pm and their conversation about the baby he was carrying, and asking for Mildred, whom Hallett referred to as Grace. He explained the confusion with her finding her father, and he said that young Florence was held back for a while and then joined her father. He stated that Head had waited till 4pm for his sons.

Wilson asked, "Was there anything at all strange either in his manner or appearance?"

Hallett replied, "None whatever. He was just as self-possessed, apparently, as I had ever seen him."

Wilson said, "There was nothing said to lead you to suspect there was anything wrong?"

"No, sir," rejoined the teacher.

There was no clarification on how Monkey avoided being collected by her father.

Henry Bryant, the last known person to have seen them all alive, was next to take the stand, and he told the court about passing the children and their father as he walked home. He mentioned specifically the baby being carried by the eldest child, and Peter holding the hand of a little boy as they walked.

PC Wells then gave his account of Mrs Head asking for his help and his subsequent discovery of the first two bodies. He corroborated Sergeant Scott's evidence of the later findings.

Battery Sergeant Major Stamp described his two sightings of Peter Head that week and how Head would often visit the mess and persuade soldiers to buy insurance policies. He spoke also of the letter and receiving the medals, which he had then handed to PC Wells. When asked by the coroner, Stamp stated he had never seen anything strange in Head's behaviour. The coroner read to the jury the letter that Stamp had received and the medals were shown. It was the postscript to that letter that would have chilled the jury the most.

'The youngsters are coming home from school, how little they think it will be their last return home.'

Cruel, deranged, psychopathic? It is difficult to label this line of words. It could, however, just be, and probably was, a matter of fact that Peter was commenting upon as he wrote the letter awaiting their return that Thursday.

Sergeant Scott was recalled to the stand and he gave some personal testimony referring to the fact that he knew Peter well, and that in recent times the insurance salesman had appeared very dejected. He described that last time when he had seen him walk past the police station, when his demeanour was such that Scott felt it necessary to comment to the workers there about Peter and the speed of his mental decline. He must have thought to himself of the possible outcome had he acted on those instincts of his and taken Peter aside, but he was also probably slightly relieved that he, in fact, was the only person to have noted any decline in behaviour. Neither Mrs Head, Sergeant Major Stamp nor the doctor had spotted or spoken of any signs of a breakdown, other than Florence speaking of his head pains.

The coroner then began to bring matters to a close. He had no further witnesses to bring, but took the opportunity to read to the court the letter that Peter had addressed to Rev Fawkes:

"... I am completely worn out with worry and reverses ..."

By 'reverses', maybe he was referring to having been knocked back so much financially after leaving the army and failing in his business.

An astute jury member, probably the church organist Edmund Brown, who had clearly done a little investigating himself, asked the coroner what date was marked on the letter and, upon being told, commented that Peter had written in the church visitors' book that day, too. Mr Wilson then read out the statement he took from Peter's widow, Florence, and commented on how curious it was that Peter would call people who committed suicide 'cowards'.

A juror, thinking there must have been some sort of argument between Florence and Peter, asked, "They had no words then, before they parted?"

Wilson replied, "No, it does not appear that they had any."

He then summed up the case and told the jury that he was sure that they would all be satisfied that Peter had murdered his six children and that the only other point was the question of his state of mind.

Wilson commented that he regretted the increase in suicides in the county and said that the crime should be as repugnant to human nature as the killing of another. He called it 'self-murder' and said that, of late, coroners' juries had been too lenient with the issue. Peter Head's suicide, however, was the only suicide in Amesbury that year.

The question of Peter's state of mind was now rather a decision for administration. Had he survived, the question of sanity would have been the deciding factor on whether or not he faced the hangman's noose. His state of mind and ability to form the malice aforethought was required to be sound enough to constitute the crime of murder.

In 1858, when Mary Ann Brough had killed her six children by the same method, she failed in doing the same to herself, so survived, but then had great difficulty talking. The jury there had labelled her insane and therefore, much to the outrage of the public at the time, she was spared the noose and confined in an asylum which, as it turned out, was ultimately a slower form of the same outcome. Similarly, Sergeant Whitworth, that other sergeant of the Artillery who murdered his six children and wife the same way in 1860, had displayed such odd behaviour immediately before, after and during the trial that he was clearly insane and he also escaped the noose. In fact, he lived in Broadmoor until his death in 1909.

Peter Robert Head was now effectively being judged for the murder of the children and the murder of himself.

Wilson continued:

"Members of the Jury, all you can do is to consider from the evidence what was the probable state of this man's mind. It did not appear that he had any motive for the crime, and naturally you will all say and feel yourselves that how is it possible that any human being could exist, however depraved, who could commit such an act as if he were in his right mind? On the other hand, you do not know, you are not experts in insanity, but it seems to me that sudden, uncontrollable impulse must have taken possession of him to cause him to do this. I believe it is within your power and in a case of this you are perfectly justified in giving your expression to your opinion and saying that this is a case of suicide or felo de se. There appears to be no motive for this crime and the man was not in want."

A jury member piped up, asking the coroner, "Were his books all right and in perfect order?"

"I believe," replied Wilson, "that there is no doubt that his books were in order. I have no evidence to that effect, but I think they were all right. I don't think there is anything further I have to say."

The jury then retired to an adjacent room of the workhouse to consider its verdict. They took some ten minutes to do so.

Mr Wilson reopened proceedings. He announced that the jury had arrived at the conclusion that Peter Robert Head had feloniously, wilfully and with malice aforethought murdered his six children. In British law, this was a finding which had only one sentence. Death.

Wilson went on to say that in the consideration of his mental state at the time, they had been struck and shocked by the face of the man in death. His expression in death had itself brought them conclusions. They came to the opinion that at the time of the crime he was, in fact, insane and that he killed himself whilst of unsound mind.

This decision, whilst rhetorical, seems contradictory to itself. If Peter was insane, then he could not have formed the intent to maliciously kill others and, had he lived, he would not have hanged for his crime. However, the large part of the insanity decision would have been reached in consideration of his subsequent suicide rather than the murders of the children. It is almost as if they were saying he was sane enough to have formed the malicious intent for the murders but insane for the suicide. The fact that he was of unsound mind when killing himself meant that he could be buried with a religious service, and with his children as he had wished.

The whole inquest lasted only two hours. Mr Read had not been called, or certainly the court reporter did not record that he was called, but he had provided Wilson with the information mentioned in relation to the probity of Head's books. They were perfect, contrary to the 'wretched state' that Peter had described them to be in in his letter to Read.

The inquest did not really answer the question that was on the lips of the whole town. The neighbours in Earls Court Road, the friends of the children at school, the soldiers who liked Peter Head, and his insurance clients. The doctor, who may have feared subsequently he missed something, the teacher who handed the children over that last time, and the police who felt Peter Head was not right in the mind but could not have foreseen such a desperate and brutal act. Why?

CHAPTER **18**

The Funeral

The inquest offered no peace to Florence, though its conclusion enabled her to bury the bodies. If she felt any anger towards her husband, she showed none publicly. She showed only grief for becoming a widow and for losing her children. She even consented to conform to Peter's last written request: to bury them all together, the murderer and the murdered. A father and his children.

They were to be buried in the cemetery in Amesbury, just a few hundred yards from the church in which Peter had written his note to Rev Fawkes.

Rev Fawkes had returned to full duties and, in fact, of the four funerals that had taken place since his own daughter's, he had officiated on two: both children of a jury member. His daughter's death had been hard and perhaps he was still too delicate to officiate at such a large and tragic funeral. Algernon Langton would conduct the Heads' funeral.

On Tuesday morning, the gravediggers got to work. It was a larger than usual task for them. From noon, the town centre became swollen with people, such was the impact on the town's population. Many of those working in the fields and shops around left their toil to show their sympathy with the family. The story had spread far and wide and appeared in most newspapers across the country and beyond.

It was a grey September day, one that was very perceptibly saying goodbye to the summer and inviting in the winter. Florence, too, was at a crossroads of her life. Saying goodbye to six of her children and her husband, while tightly holding the hand of her surviving child and either wondering if anybody would notice the gradual swelling of her belly or just realising it herself. Also, she now had to work out how to pay for her life. Whereas the financial hardship Peter was worried about was more in his head than in his pocket, now, thanks to him, it was suddenly a reality for Florence.

To attend the funeral was too much for Florence. She and Monkey did not go.

A group of people gathered by the entrance of the workhouse where the bodies had remained. In the mortuary, each body had been placed in its own coffin. These were brought outside and positioned on the biers as the procession got itself in order.

The monochrome of the grey day was temporarily relieved with the arrival of the Royal Artillery in their dress uniforms. Their dark blue tunics with red piping and collars, gold braiding and gold sergeant stripes contrasted with the dull, dirty smocks of the field workers and drab suits of the shop workers.

The evil of the act had not deterred Peter Head's friends and comrades from attending and paying him and his children their last respects.

The police headed the parade. Superintendent Longstone, his grey mutton chops reflecting the mood, took up the front with Sergeant Scott, wearing his custodian helmet. His black moustache was as part of his 1905 uniform, as it was for all the soldiers present. Next in line was a hand-bier, the hand-drawn hearse of the time – a platform of wood upon four carriage wheels with a handle to the front to pull the vehicle. Mounted on top, and covered in wreaths of white flowers, was the dark wooden coffin of Peter Robert Head. This was drawn by bowler-hatted men from the Prudential and escorted by twenty-two sergeants of the Royal Artillery. Behind that came a four-wheeled horse-drawn vehicle. Six small white coffins sat upon it, also completely adorned with white flower wreaths. Walking alongside to keep his nieces and nephews company was the only family member present, Albert King.

The streets were crowded with onlookers, and their shock and sorrow was so palpable as the mournful silent procession made its way along Salisbury Street. Soldiers along the street stood to attention and, as the procession turned from Salisbury Street towards the cemetery, there was a group of sixty to seventy soldiers who saluted as the body of former Sergeant Major Head passed by.

Rev Langton met the procession at the entrance to the cemetery. He conducted the ceremony as the seven coffins lay next to the single grave that was dug to hold them all together in perpetuity. Seven coffins that, if empty, could well have fitted together like Russian dolls, such was the contrast in sizes. The tiny white coffin of Freddie, only nine months old, was the last to be gently laid into the ground. This was the last straw for many in attendance, and lots of onlookers around the edge of the cemetery were in tears. The children had been placed in the ground three deep next to their father. Three coffins wide was the space they would share for eternity. He murdered them and he got to stay with them forever.

As the service ended, many of those people present came to the edge of the grave and dropped in some earth or flowers, some with labels dedicated to the children.

There were several large floral tributes. Florence had left two, each with a note attached.

*'To my dear children from their sorrowing mother –
"Suffer little children to come unto me"'*

and

'To my dear husband, from his sorrowing wife'

Despite what he had done, she still expressed to him the love of a widow, and always would. It is difficult to assess the sincerity of her words to Peter. Her emotions must have been all over the place, and as six of her children were buried, she held the hand of her second eldest and felt a twinge in her belly from her youngest. Her family would never hear her say a bad word about Peter.

There was another wreath which said, *'From old comrades and friends with love and sincere sympathy'*. This could well have come from the Scottish regiment he had left behind.

A newspaper reported that one wreath said, *'To dear little Teddy from his godfather. With heartfelt sympathy'*. This was certainly for the baby Freddie and was either a mistake by the newspaper or the child was called Teddy by his friends. It is difficult to say who Frederick George Head's godfather was. It was possibly a neighbour from Durrington who had baptised his own daughter the same day as the Heads baptised Frederick. They possibly named him after that neighbour, Frederick George Lawes.

Sergeant Major Stamp's contingent sent a wreath: *'For the dear little children, a token of affection from their father's friends in the 28th RFA Brigade'*. Notably for the children, not for their friend.

Mrs Hallett had arranged a floral tribute from the school, though the school logbook does not mention any children being allowed time away to attend the funeral, nor does any newspaper mention either Mr or Mrs Hallett going. The wreath read:

'In sad and deepest sympathy and affectionate remembrance of the six little Heads, from their teachers and companions at Amesbury School'

There was a similar wreath from the students and teachers of Durrington School.

A card was left from their school friends Berty, Albert and Ethel Wootton. Ethel was Monkey's age, and though she would live a long life into her nineties, she would also experience her own grief when two of her three sons were killed in the Second World War.

Slowly, the crowds slipped away and left the six children and their father to spend their first night in their forever home, deep in the cold Wiltshire ground. A reporter from the *Salisbury Times* had attended the inquest and funeral and made the only public record of the event. The article was replicated in newspapers across the entire nation. Even back in Mey, it was realised that the murderer was their Sergeant Major Head: the man who had commanded their volunteers and who had entertained them so often and spent several genial years amongst their population. All reports of Peter were positive, except, of course, with reference to him killing the children, which was referred to more often as a tragic event than the inexplicable brutal cold-blooded slaughter it actually was.

For a short while, sorrow and anguish presided over the town of Amesbury. The following week, the harvest festival attracted far fewer attendees in church and lower donations than in previous years. The 'tragedy' was blamed as a cause of this unusual indifference.

CHAPTER 19

Florence's Next Steps

As Florence did not attend the funeral, cards and flowers were her proxy. It was clear that the whole town had come out in great sympathy and sorrow for her and Peter's surviving daughters.

The day after the funeral, Florence knew there needed to be changes, and quickly. She knew that people would be crossing the road to avoid having to express their sympathy personally, and that she would forever be looked upon in Amesbury with pitying eyes. What is more, the subject of her swelling pregnancy would cause more stir, more rumour and quite possibly an amount of conjecture.

Young Elsie, Monkey, never went back to Amesbury School, and the Halletts continued as if nothing had happened. There is an entry by Hallett in the school logbook that simply records, 'Florence and Grace Head are dead'. There was no record of Elsie leaving the school.

Very soon after the events, Florence packed up their few belongings. With her husband dead, she had no ties in Wiltshire and now very little income. She needed support and she did not want to raise another child in the place where six had been murdered. Her parents were still alive, and home is where she headed.

She returned to her native Worcester and rented a small house in Whinfield Road. Two terraces of houses still stand on opposite sides on the west end of the road by the New Inn pub, mirroring each other. Grantham Villas and Granville Terrace. Florence lived in the former.

Florence had the matter of Peter's probate to sort out. Despite any notions of a preconceived intention to die, he had not considered making a will, nor leaving any kind of official instructions to his wife. He died intestate, and the letters of administration drawn up at the Principal Probate Registry awarded Florence the estate he left, which was, after tax, £81 15 shillings and 6 pence. This is an equivalent of over £12,600 today. Peter was far from being on the bread line or suffering such poverty as to require the murder of his children.

Florence clearly did not want to be reliant on a man, not again. She may well have drawn strength remembering the ladies she had served back in the 1890s, while in service for Miss Braysher, but wherever it came from, she knew she must fend for herself. Her pregnancy was progressing, and even though she had, up to very recently, six other children, the prospect of a newborn in her circumstances was not the best for her. Finding employment in her condition was one thing, and also working while caring for children was another.

The nine-year-old Monkey was also being her characterful tearaway, and Florence took a decision that seems somewhat strange today. Having lost six children, it would seem natural today to keep the surviving one close by, but Florence sent Monkey away to a boarding school. Not actually a boarding school, but to an orphanage. Perhaps Monkey's presence and her resemblance to the lost ones was an unbearable reminder for Florence.

The 'Charity of the Royal Artillery', which was run by Colonel Hutchinson, was particularly proactive in its assistance to widows. Florence had turned to them for help.

It was probably Colonel Hutchinson's suggestion to send Monkey to the Sisters of Bethany Orphanage in Bournemouth. He had arranged for orphans to go there in the past.

Colonel Hutchinson agreed to finance Monkey's stay, and she was admitted into the orphanage on 1st February, 1906.

A little over four months after losing her father and six siblings, Monkey's world was again turned on its head, and she was left in the care of the Sisters of Bethany. A place of rules and religion. Having lost her father and siblings so violently, and probably very conscious of her own narrow escape, the little girl now lost her mother, too. Ironically, once at the orphanage, Monkey was living just over a mile away from St Peter's Church, where her father had been looked after when he was of a similar age; both of them sent away by their mothers because of the death of their fathers.

The Anglican order the Sisters of Bethany established its orphanage whilst Peter Head was a chorister in Bournemouth in the 1870s. Built in Church Road, modern-day St Clement's Road, the building could house one hundred orphans (or not, in Monkey's case) who were between two and ten years old on their admission. In a strictly Christian upbringing, the girls were trained for a life in service. Skills such as embroidery, laundry and housework were an add-on to a basic education. It was a disciplined institution and not one into which someone with Monkey's temperament would fit easily. Probably with fits of guilt as well as loneliness and feelings of abandonment, here Monkey honed the skill she had already shown an aptitude for – survival.

With her only child now in an institution, Florence had to turn her attention to one more thing before the imminent birth of her new child. Only two days after Monkey's admittance into the orphanage, on 3rd February, 1906, Elizabeth Head, Peter's ailing mother, was admitted one more time into the

Marylebone Infirmary. The news of the death of her son and six grandchildren could have been the catalyst to accelerate her already speedy physical decline. With Florence at her new Worcestershire address named as her next of kin in the admission papers and not Peter, it is clear that Elizabeth was aware that at least her son was dead. It is likely that she also knew of the entire incident, so ubiquitous were the newspaper reports. It also shows the care that Florence took to keep in contact with her mother-in-law.

Now very heavily pregnant, Florence Head moved to London one month later. She took lodgings at 63 Kennington Park Road, Newington. An institution called Mildmay Haven ran this as a refuge for single or 'fallen' mothers, so by staying there, Florence had tapped into another charitable organisation to help her out.

Florence visited Elizabeth in the Marylebone Infirmary. Elizabeth was getting frailer and more unwell, suffering from rheumatism and exhaustion. Florence would do what she could to make her more comfortable, but little was left to be done to prolong her life. The care at the infirmary was not great, and Elizabeth had developed gaping bed sores which inevitably would have become infected. April, 1906, was a month of great suffering for Elizabeth, and she died on the 30th with Florence by her side. On 1st May, she was laid to rest in Hendon Cemetery. There is no stone and the paperwork states she was sixty-six, when she was more likely seventy-two. Elizabeth had always had an imprecise relationship with her age.

Just two weeks later, Peter Head's last child was born. Florence took herself into the General Lying-in Hospital in York Road, London, a hospital largely used by single destitute women. Frances Mary Head was born on 15th May, 1906.

A little girl who should have been welcomed into the arms of her funny, loving father and excited three sisters, four brothers and half-sister in their crowded rural cottage surrounded by laughter, love, song and security, was taken back temporarily to the refuge with Florence. Frances Mary Head was born into a lonely world on the verge of turmoil, into a family hanging on for survival. The legacy of her siblings' murders immediately scarred her the moment she entered the world.

Since the death of most of her family, Florence had acted decisively and harshly, but with little choice. She had accepted charity wherever she could find it, knowing that it would be temporary and that she needed just to get through the immediacy of the problems that the tragedy had placed upon her. Placing Monkey into the orphanage at the expense of the Royal Artillery Charity meant she had one mouth less to feed whilst trying to sort herself out. Then she had used a refuge to stay in in London while she helped her mother-in-law in her last days, before giving birth in a hospital for 'fallen' or single mothers. Florence knew how to find the help she needed, but she now had to earn a living, another demanding thing to manage with a baby. Once recovered from her eighth birth, the thirty-five-year-old Florence returned to Worcester with her new child, where she could find some assistance from her family.

It is more than likely that baby Frances actually went straight to Florence's mother, Emily King. By the time Frances had turned a year old in May, 1907, Florence had enrolled as a midwife and was training for the new Central Midwives Board (CMB) examination to qualify into that profession. Maybe inspired by her recent experiences in London, this appeared to her as a way ahead in term of career and income. Whilst training, she lived in the Nurses Institute Home in

Worcester, so it seems unlikely that baby Frances was with her.

Here, Florence shows such a contradiction of character. One way of coping with losing so many of her own children was to help bring the babies of others into the world. Paradoxically, she seems to have turned her back on her own young, shocked and grieving surviving daughter, Monkey, and her reliant newborn, Frances.

When Frances turned two years old, she became eligible for admittance into the Sisters of Bethany Orphanage, and on 4th May, 1908, Florence packed her off to Bournemouth. The £11 a year cost of her attendance at the orphanage was also paid for by Colonel Hutchinson of the Royal Artillery Charity. With both daughters now safely in the orphanage, Florence could concentrate on her training to look after the birth of other people's children, without the constant reminder of not being able to protect her own.

After qualifying, Florence Head worked as a district midwife and nurse from her lodgings in Hurst Lane as part of the Worcester Nursing Association. For a while she covered the area of Martin Hussingtree, and no doubt she kept herself busy in the role into which she had thrown herself. Little had she expected, whilst the wife of a Sergeant Major of the Royal Artillery, following him across the country from post to post and becoming a mother of a rapidly growing family, that she would end up living alone pursuing her own vocation.

Filling in the 1911 census form on 3rd April, Florence would have considered this past and one can only wonder what went through her mind as she furnished the form with the information that she had been married thirteen years and had eight children, six of whom had died.

The Royal Artillery Charity continued to pay for Monkey's and Frances's education at the Sisters of Bethany. For Elsie, the characteristics that had earned her the nickname Monkey almost certainly got her into a few scrapes. The abandonment she must have felt, mixed with her excitable and repressed adventurous nature and un-counselled grief, must have made these defining years of growth a very difficult time. Family oral history tells that this was not a happy time for Monkey, and that it included several incarcerations in various small rooms of the orphanage. How much interaction the two young sisters had with each other during their stay at the home is unclear, but this is where their relationship would have grown if it did, and not in a family home, although for Frances, however, this was really the only family home she would have known.

Monkey must have been very relieved when, on 5th September, 1913, aged seventeen, she finally left the institution. With mixed emotions because of leaving her seven-year-old sister behind, she returned to her mother. The orphanage recorded that she left to spend some time with her mother before going into a life of service.

With Monkey's return, perhaps Florence realised that there was some sort of comfort to be had amongst her own. Two years later, at Monkey's behest, on 15th August, 1915, the approach to the tenth anniversary of the murders, Florence sent for Frances, who was nine years old and had been in the orphanage since she was two. Florence, it seems, had settled into a sufficient routine of work and income that she could cope with the return of her two daughters, but the insecurities that Frances had absorbed were deep and lasting. Going home must have been a huge culture shock to the institutionalised child.

Britain had sunk into the horrors of the First World War, and it is quite likely that Florence would have lent a hand at the convalescent homes established in stately homes in the area. It is difficult to know what Monkey did in these late teenage years, as there were no records of the 'Land Army', but it is likely that she played her part in the significant female contribution to the running of the country during the war.

During this time, Florence would have reflected more than once that, had her sons survived, at least two of them would have been of the age to fight in the war. One or both may have perished, like several of their school friends from Amesbury did. Notably, three of the jurors sitting on the Head murder inquest lost children in the First World War.

On 14th April, 1919, Florence's mother, Emily King, died. She was seventy-four years old and had suffered from heart disease. Florence's younger sister, Mary Lillian Clegg, who was with Emily at the time of her death, registered the event that day.

Emily's death was a catalyst for change, but any known reason is lost to the mist of time. In 1919, twenty-three-year-old Monkey, who now used the Christian name of Elsa on her passport, moved to France, where she went to work initially as a governess for the Countesse Kergorlay. At some stage, and it is likely to have been in France, she also trained as a nurse.

That year, Florence took a job as a district nurse in Llandrindod Wells, and she and Frances moved to that thriving spa town in mid-Wales. They lived first in Temple Avenue, probably in hospital accommodation, and then moved to a small, terraced cottage at 4 Wellington Terrace. Aged fifteen, Frances left education and secured a job as a draper's assistant in the Central Wales Emporium, a large, elegant department store somewhat incongruous with its more rural surroundings.

CHAPTER 20

Amy's Life

After the murders, Peter Head's surviving family had spread thinly across the country and apart from each other. By 1908, as we have seen, the two youngest girls, Monkey, twelve years old, and Frances, two, lived under the care of the religious doctrines of the Sisters of Bethany in Bournemouth, and their half-sister, Amy Edith Head, now twenty-one, was working in service in London.

Ironically, Amy was the real orphan among her surviving half-siblings. She also had the struggles of her disability. The difficulties faced at this time by a young lady with one leg cannot be underestimated, and working in service as a cook meant she was constantly standing up, often using one arm to do the work and one to hold the crutch that helped keep her on her remaining foot. Amy's lifelong aversion to wearing a prosthetic leg must have put a lot of physical pressure on her, but she only ever used a crutch. Not the easiest way to navigate a kitchen, but one that she managed efficiently. Amy, like her half-sister, Monkey, was a survivor, too. She was very conscious of her missing leg, and whilst she did what she could to disguise it, she did not allow it to define her, and she worked as hard as anyone.

There is no record of any contact being maintained between Amy, her stepmother Florence or her half-sisters. It does seem that if there was any contact between them, as the years passed and both sisters strove to make a living, this drifted and stopped. Certainly, Amy's children and then grandchildren were unaware she had a stepmother until the murders were discovered much later.

In 1911, Amy was working in Arngask Road, Catford, as a domestic servant at the home of Philip Morehen, assistant to the Admiral in Charge at the Admiralty.

After leaving the Morehen family, Amy remained in service, and by 1921 was living in a house in Bellsize Park, Hampstead, where she worked as a cook for a recently widowed fifty-seven-year-old Jewish lady called Esther Ellison. During the shadow of the First World War, Esther's husband Joseph Eisenman, a toy merchant from Germany, had anglicised their surname to Ellison. Joseph had died in 1920.

There is no evidence or knowledge within the family as to whether or not Amy and Frances had met each other, or even that Amy knew of her existence. We know that Amy knew Monkey because Amy was staying with the Head family in Scotland in 1901. It does appear that the turmoil of events in 1905 and the starburst in terms of the roads that each took afterwards to survive resulted in Amy losing contact with her stepmother, Florence, and her half-sister, Monkey. It is often the way with humans that meeting someone who has some kind of attachment to a traumatic incident that results in deep feelings, serves to remind you of those feelings, and therefore avoidance and non-contact is the path of least resistance. Letters may have passed between them initially, but Amy's children were never made aware that she had half-siblings.

In many ways, Amy Head had the most to overcome. Growing and working and thriving with one leg took an enormous amount of effort. She had lost her mother before she could remember and lived with her grandparents in Kent from a very young age. She was short of three years old when her grandfather died, and so was brought up, along with her uncles and aunts, by her grandmother, Fanny Tanner.

She was living with her father, stepmother, and half-siblings in Scotland in 1901 when the census was taken, and this indicates that she probably lived with the Tanners for some considerable time until space became compromised. By the time she was seventeen years old, she had moved to Portsmouth, where she lived with Albert King, her step-uncle. It was said that when she was told of the death of her father and siblings, she went grey overnight. Whilst probably a metaphoric exaggeration, she would obviously have been highly shocked and traumatised just at the point when she entered adult life.

Working in service meant she lived where she worked, and that work was often long hours split across a longer day. Her ability to have any kind of social life was restricted by those hours, her disability, and the times in which she lived. She remained single into her late thirties.

Returning to Kent, her final job as a live-in cook was at the home of a colonel, and it was in Kent where she met Ernest George Flavell.

At twenty-three, Ernest George Flavell was significantly younger than Amy's thirty-eight years when they married in St Barnabas Church on 22nd October, 1926. Their wedding photograph shows Ernest in a suit as he stands smiling proudly above Amy, who is sitting on a chair in her white dress and veil, with her crutch hidden well away from shot. Her life changed completely with her marriage, and at last she had a family of her own. Her cousin, Herbert Tanner, was one of the witnesses.

Amy and Ernest had two daughters: Avis Margaret Amy, born in 1927, and Hazel Joyce, born in 1930. They lived in Peabody Road, Farnborough. In 1939, Ernest was still in the Royal Engineers, working as a stoker.

Ernest was utterly devoted to, and protective towards Amy, and very loving towards their children and grandchildren. He was the softness to Amy's slightly more Victorian taciturn nature. Whilst he would have the children jumping all over him, she kept a very slight physical distance, through fear of hurting her stump just above her missing knee. However, she did give her time generously and enjoyed teaching them. Amy was accomplished at making artificial flowers from crêpe paper and was a skilled embroiderer. She could also be strict about things that reflected her own very Victorian upbringing by her grandmother, and matters such as eating in the street were, to Amy, heinous offences. Very aware of how she looked, she even dressed smartly to watch the television, not quite understanding that it was a one-way medium.

Being so protective towards Amy, Ernest demonstrated that he knew her past and would quickly deflect any talk about her childhood. When one of the daughters once mentioned an interest in trying to find Amy's mother's grave, Ernest told her not to meddle in her past as it would upset her. That was a clear reference to the fact that he knew about that past, and that it still affected Amy very much.

Over the years, the incipient notion that there was a dark secret about their grandfather grew in the Flavell girls, and having overheard some talk, they suspected that there could be a suicide involved. That was the extent of their suspicions. Amy never let on.

Amy defied the very difficult start she had in life by firstly working hard and learning to thrive against the odds, and then by living a long and happy life, loved by those around her. The cloud that hovered above her remained omnipresent, but she kept it at bay and lived her life, providing a solid home for her children and grandchildren. She only ever said kind and loving things about Peter Head and had told her children that the last time she had seen him they had visited Winchester Cathedral together. This could well have been on the way back from London on the Wednesday of that fateful week. The way she spoke was as if in her mind she judged her father as she had always found him, and not by the last act he had perpetrated. Perhaps a distance from Florence and Monkey kept a distance from the truth for her.

Amy died in 1975 aged eighty-seven, having lived some sixty-two years longer than her mother and eighty-six longer than her youngest sibling. Her children still knew something was not right in their history, but nothing more was discovered until many years later, when Avis was diagnosed with terminal cancer and asked her daughter, Liz, to find out what happened to her grandfather. It was only then, with the purchase of the death certificate, that they discovered how Peter had died and that he had murdered the half-siblings they never knew their grandmother had.

CHAPTER 21

Frances Joan Head

Frances never really experienced life in a proper family home environment. Being brought up in the orphanage and not returning to her mother until she was nine would have instilled a different outlook within her from that of many children.

It is not known where Frances met William Mandeville Cotterell, but it was some time in the early 1920s. He was a corporal in the Royal Corps of Signals. Cotterell was already very well known within running circles. He broke records and, amongst other titles, was the National and Army Champion at cross-country running. He was ubiquitous in the sports newspapers throughout the 1920s and much of the 1930s. William was a charismatic man, a joker, and by all accounts a bit of a lady's man. In 1925, he was stationed in Oxford temporarily while attending a course there. Frances and William married in Oxford on 25th November, 1925. Their marriage certificate states they were both twenty-three years old, when, in fact, Frances was actually only nineteen years old.

Their marriage was the first official record of Frances using the name Frances Joan Head rather than using her birth middle name of Mary. Where and why she adopted the name of Joan and dropped Mary is not known, but from this point onwards she was actually known in the family as

Joan, and all documentation, official or otherwise, refers to her as Joan or Frances Joan. It is possible this was what she was known as at the orphanage and that she kept it. We will call her Joan from now on.

In March, 1927, William had come third in the National Cross-country Championships held in Beaconsfield. A couple of months later, on 10th June, 1927, Joan and William had a daughter, Pamela Mandeville Cotterell. Pamela was born in Durham. Only a week or so later, William won the three-mile cross-country event at the Army Athletic Championships, completing the course in 14 minutes 59 seconds. Head forwards, shoulders hunched was his recognisable distinctive and winning style.

The Royal Corps of Signals was posted to Bulford in Wiltshire. Right back to where Peter Robert Head had gone to sell his insurance and drink at the mess. On 28th May, 1929, nearly twenty-four years after the murders, William and Joan had a son, who they named Peter Mandeville Cotterell.

Peter Robert Head's grandson, named after him, was born a spitting distance from where his mother's siblings had been killed. To be named after her murdering father suggests perhaps a lack of full knowledge on Joan's part or ambivalence at this time. It was while serving here, and not from Joan, that William first heard about the murders while drinking in an Amesbury pub with his soldier mates. What Joan even knew at this stage is sketchy, though it is possible she learnt a lot from Monkey whilst at the orphanage as she grew up. It is highly doubtful it was something she could discuss with Florence, and it became an unspoken awareness that something dark had befallen them all. Regardless of the events or knowledge of them, Peter Robert Head continued to be spoken of kindly within the family, and now Peter Cotterell, the first boy born since the murders, was given his name.

While Pamela was told that her mother's siblings died of a plague, Peter was later once told that one day Monkey returned from shopping to find the bodies of all her brothers and sisters on their lawn. Perhaps that's how his young mind remembered the images he conjured up after being told.

In 1930, William Cotterell experienced tendon injuries and he could not compete as often nor with such winning effect. On his return to competitions in 1932, his form was not as successful. Younger men were beating him. That year saw the couple have another son, John Robert Cotterell. Another reference to Joan's father with the 'Robert'. The child was known as Bobby.

William left the army and became a caretaker at the Artillery Barracks, The Green, near West Ham. After the Second World War had started, however, he rejoined, becoming Quarter Master Sergeant Instructor in the Army Physical Training Corps. He continued training soldiers throughout the duration of the war.

Joan, who was not born at the time of her siblings' murders, was about to experience some of the grief she did not see her mother experience. In April, 1939, William and Joan were living in the barracks at West Ham. Their two sons, Bobby and Peter, were playing on the roofs of some outbuildings when little Bobby Cotterell, only six years old, slipped and fell to the ground, landing on his back.

He died shortly afterwards as a result of the fall. The grief and shock of that moment stayed with Peter Cotterell all his life, even though he was himself only twelve at the time. Perhaps there was some kind of unspoken survivor's empathy between him and Monkey that bonded their relationship later.

Though Bobby's death introduced Joan to the grief that her mother held, it is unlikely that she would have turned to Florence for comfort, although Florence herself must have felt the loss of her grandson acutely too. Additionally, Joan and William's already tenuous relationship would not survive the resulting grief, and the small nucleus of their family unit would run out of steam. William kept running. They buried Bobby in the City of London cemetery.

In 1941, aged thirty-seven, William was still competing at a high level and came thirteenth in a field of over two hundred for the Aldershot Command Cross-country Championship.

During the war, Pamela was evacuated to Wales to live with her grandmother, Florence Head, in Llandrindod Wells. This was probably not particularly convenient for Florence, who now had no family commitments but plenty of professional ones. Pamela was twelve at the time and did not find her grandmother to be particularly friendly towards her. She told her own children later how she fell off a bicycle and grazed herself, but was not cleaned up by her grandmother nurse. After staying there a short time, the young Pamela decided to return to London and, plucky as ever and under her own steam, made her way back to the capital, which looked dramatically different on her return. It was 10th October, 1940, the day after St Paul's Cathedral had been bombed, and all the underground stations were in use as bomb shelters with no underground trains available for travel. Pamela managed to find her way to Woolwich and then found a ferry up the Thames to Sidcup. When she returned home, Joan's surprise turned to anger directed at her own mother for the apparent neglect to clean up the wounds Pamela had sustained when falling from her bike. Peter later recalled his mother having to break his sister's skin to pick out the gravel. With William being busy in the Army and Joan working for the Government, Pamela was given to a young family to be looked after, but, after a bout of sickness, she was put in the workhouse, before William tracked her down. This time, she remained with her parents for a while.

The turmoil of war ran parallel to the instability and spectre of grief within the Cotterell family. Joan worked as a civil servant in the War Office and William was training soldiers. Still raw with grief from the death of their son, their relationship broke down towards the end of the war, and certainly by 1946, they had split irrevocably. William briefly lived back with his parents and Joan moved to a rented flat.

Joan's somewhat narcissistic nature had shown itself by now, and as her two surviving children grew, she insisted that they called her by her name 'Joan', as she did not want people to know she was old enough to have children of that age.

At sixteen, Pamela trained as a hairdresser at Harvey Nicholls in London, and at a dance in Covent Garden in 1944, she met an American soldier called John Ahearn. Their relationship flourished. He was an aeroplane mechanic, and even Joan liked him. In her capacity within the War Office, she was able to arrange leave passes for him from time to time. John returned to the USA after the war and Pamela saved up some money. On 19th March, 1946, ten months after the end of the Second World War and while she was still only eighteen years old, she went to London and obtained a visa to travel to America. A week later, she took the train up to Prestwick in Scotland, where, on 19th March, she boarded a flight to Clinton, Connecticut, where she declared her intention to reside permanently in the United States and live with her fiancé, John J. Ahearn. She had never felt particularly close to her mother, who, like her own mother, was not particularly maternal, and at eighteen she sought a new life away from her parents in a place she had never visited. There she stayed and brought up her own family in the way she wanted. Pamela and John married ten days after her arrival in the country in April, 1946. She became actively involved in the community and held a number of civil offices. She was able to provide the affection to her children that was not given to her.

William Cotterell finally retired from the Army for a second time in 1946, and after he and Joan were divorced, he married Daisy Kitchener in 1949. They lived together for several years in Eynham Road, Hammersmith.

Joan continued working as a civil servant, and probably related to this, she met a Polish refugee called Zbignew Marian Klaudiusz Zakrzewski. Known as Ben, he was part of the huge diaspora escaping the German invasion of Poland and was considered stateless. The family recalls that Ben had been in a concentration camp during the war and suffered greatly at the hands of the Nazis. No records in the Simon Wiesenthal Centre can corroborate this; however, it is clear his journey was great and traumatic during those years. Ben decided to settle in America, and he sailed there on the *Queen Elizabeth* in May, 1951, landing in New York. Joan followed him a few months later and they settled in New Haven, Connecticut, close to her daughter, Pamela, and her family.

CHAPTER 22

Monkey in France and Joan in America

In the 1920s, Monkey had become a nurse in France and started working for a dentist called Dr Leon Monier. In 1926, she lived on the outskirts of Paris with a fellow nurse called Isobel MacCulloch, who had been in the French Red Cross during the First World War, being awarded the British Victory Medal.

In 1936, Monkey was still working as a nurse and, at forty years old, was living alone in the chic Batignolles area of Paris. It is not clear what the nature of her relationship with Dr Monier was, but she worked for him for many years. During that time, she would holiday in the small town of Saint-Pierre-d'Autils, some 85km north-west of Paris.

The rise of national socialism in neighbouring Germany did not encourage her to return to England, so she remained in France and would have witnessed the invasion of Paris by the German Army as the occupation took hold in June, 1940. The Germans took over the governance of the city and life became a more dangerous affair.

In about 1942, during the occupation, Monkey married a dentist called Lucien Marc Mathiot. It may have been a marriage of convenience, and certainly has been called that by those who remember her. Certainly, it would have benefited her to have a French name at this time. When and where exactly they married, or indeed if they did, is unclear. A record in France cannot be found. However, all subsequent official documentation in relation to both of them is written as if they had been legally married. They moved to Saint-Pierre-d'Autils and lived in Le Verger, the house opposite St Pierre Church, where Monkey had holidayed. This had been built a couple of years before her father's birth and contained a large garden which was walled along the approaching road to the village. Elsa enjoyed pottering about and developing her garden. It was likely that Lucien and Elsa had bought the house then, but possible that it belonged initially to Dr Monier. Certainly their relationship with Dr Monier was a close one, and when he died that year he was buried in the small cemetery at the entrance to the village.

The German occupation of France rendered communications with England impossible for most civilians. Consequently, Florence had no news from her daughter.

In 1939, at the beginning of the war, Nurse Florence Head was living in lodgings in a house called Singleton in Temple Drive, Llandrindod Wells, Wales. She lived with Frances Emily Davies, a widow, sister of Dr Bevan, the first Bishop of Swansea and Brecon. I wonder if living here in a household of just women brought back memories of living in Bristol with Amelia Ann Blanford Edwards and Ellen Braysher so many years earlier before her own marriage? There she had seen a household of women flourish without need for a man.

By the beginning of the Second World War, most of the twenty-two nurses of the Llandrindod Wells Nursing Association had a telephone in their home and access to a motor car. How alien it would have seemed had Peter Head been able to see his widow now. No children around her in the kitchen, but driving a car and speaking on a telephone, responsible for nursing and midwifery over a large area. A world away. Six little lives away.

In 1942, after enquiring through the Red Cross, Florence was reassured that her daughter was safe and 'fairly' well. Florence was also informed that Elsa (Monkey) had married. This was the first she knew of it.

The war raged on, but she heard nothing from Monkey. Florence, desperate for information, wrote again in June, 1944, ten days after the D-Day allied invasion of France. She wrote to the Civilian Enquiries section of the Supreme Headquarters Allied Expeditionary Force, asking for Elsa to be found now that Paris was liberated. Florence offered to pay for her transit and to cover any costs incurred by her being back in England so that she 'was not a drain on the state'. She did not know that Elsa was living in Saint-Pierre-d'Autils, which had not yet been liberated. Florence had not seen her eldest surviving child for several years and was now desperately trying to establish if she was actually still alive.

'Will you please give me some hope that something can be done to bring her over here at a future date and any advice would be welcome.'

Here we see a different and warmer Florence than the one we conjure up when we learn of her putting her surviving daughters into the orphanage. A Florence who is worried about losing a seventh child. It shows that at the time of the murders she had had no choice and was maybe acting like an automaton, disabled in grief, distraughtly trying to forge a future for all of them, but having to take such desperate measures to do so. Here she is, almost forty years later, trying to use the available systems and organisations to find news of the daughter who she so nearly lost all those years ago. Offering the state her own hard-earned funding to do so. It is a letter of love in not so many words. She does not want to think that this daughter has joined the six siblings, when she was so lucky not to have left school with them that day in 1905. This is the trying to hold her close we would have expected to see then, that Florence had been unable to do.

With the marriage that the Red Cross had told Florence about, Monkey's name was now Madame Elsa Mathiot. The marriage had served to disguise her English name, which was advantageous once German soldiers occupied their village, some of whom were billeted in Le Verger with the Mathiots. The nearby city of Vernon was a strong enclave of the German occupying army. Earlier on in the war, there had been talk in the village that Monkey would be given up if things heated up, but she countered that by warning people that, if that occurred, she would tell the Germans they were Jewish. They all kept quiet. Germans occupied the Mathiots' house and never discovered Monkey was English. Elsa became more accepted and helped out in the village as a general nurse, patching up people and helping the elderly. Vernon and the surrounding areas were some of the last places of that part of France to be evacuated by the Germans after the Allies advanced south from Normandy in June, 1944. When they left, the Germans trashed Elsa and Lucien's house. The occupants of Saint-Pierre-d'Autils did survive the war, however, and the stress of occupation or threat of being caught in the crossfire from any combatants was over. The village was able to return to being a quiet rural community.

Monkey had survived again. In the 1946 French census, she is listed as being French.

Florence retired from nursing in 1946 at seventy-five years old. In 1953, she joined Monkey and Lucien in France. She stayed for some considerable time with them, where she forged a great friendship with their housekeeper, Titian. There is a photograph of an elderly-looking Florence with

Titian by the front door of Le Verger, and another of Florence sitting in a chair in the driveway with the church behind her.

On 21st March, 1953, Joan, using her real first name and newly married name, Frances Zakrzewski, boarded the weekly luxury liner RMS *Queen Elizabeth* in New York and disembarked in Cherbourg. In France, the three survivors of Peter Head's awful actions were together once more. Joan left for England in May. She had tried to persuade her son, Peter, to bring forward his wedding, planned for August, but his and fiancé Barbara's arrangements were firmly in place, and Joan was in England at the wrong time. Her relationship with Peter had never been great, but she arrived laden with gifts for the soon-to-be-married couple, with new bed linen and nightwear for Barbara. Barbara found Joan friendly enough, although a little intimidating at times and with an aura of sadness about her. Joan left England at the end of that month and once more joined the RMS *Queen Elizabeth* for the journey back to New York and on to New Haven, Connecticut, and Ben.

After Peter and Barbara were married that August, they detoured on their way home to get changed for their honeymoon and visited the cemetery where Peter's little brother, Bobby, was buried. In a tearful visit, they left the bride's bouquet on Bobby's grave.

For their honeymoon, they flew their motorbike to France and went on tour. They had intended their first stop would be for just one night. Joan had insisted that they must visit her sister, Monkey, so that is exactly what they did. They reached the village of Saint-Pierre-d'Autils and, stopping the motorcycle by a wall to get their bearings, they heard a voice from behind saying, "I think they're there." It was Monkey, but to them it sounded very much like Joan. They ended up staying several days. Barbara found both Florence and Monkey to be full of fun, talkative, and great to spend time with. Florence was always joking with her, and despite the years that had passed, demonstrated a bit of barrack-room humour. Monkey had a garden full of fruit trees, one of which was the slightly laxative-effecting Medlar fruit, which Florence called 'open arses'. She also laughed at how Peter would 'crack his nuts' when he used his clutch lever to open walnuts. Monkey made them very welcome and would make meals they had never had before. For instance, omelette was not something Barbara had experienced. Before Barbara died many years later, she wrote a wonderful account of her life, and in this she spoke with great warmth of Florence and Monkey.

In 1958, Florence, now eighty-seven, who once would have travelled by horse and cart and old steam trains, took an Air France flight from Paris to New York and travelled onwards to Connecticut, where she was reunited with Joan, staying with her and Ben.

Monkey enjoyed having Florence living with her and was upset when she finally left, blaming Joan for persuading her to do so. Fifty-three years had passed since the murders and the chaotic aftermath that so defined them all, and once again Monkey was being separated from her mother.

In keeping with Joan's self-conscious personality, she persuaded Ben to change their Polish surname. In November, 1958, they became Marion Robert Benan and Frances Joan Benan.

Pamela's daughter, Sheila, who was quite young at the time, recalls meeting Florence in 1958. She and her brothers, Mike and Tim, visited Joan's apartment with their mother, who was very pregnant at the time. Sheila remembers Florence referring to them as 'brats', and on seeing Pamela in her advanced state of pregnancy, saying

something to the effect of, "*Oh another one, how disgusting.*"
As a result, the American great-grandchildren did not visit
her again, though she remained in America for some while.
This interaction tainted their opinion of Florence to the
point that they thought she was somewhat deranged. They
recall that Florence complained of the journey to America,
too, and how she had not been treated as well as she had
thought befitted her station. This kind of attitude may explain
why Monkey sometimes referred to Florence as the 'Queen
Mother'.

Sheila found Florence to be very stand-offish, as one who
felt that she should be treated exceptionally highly, like some
sort of royalty. Her reaction to children and particularly a
pregnant woman is certainly incongruous with her nursing
and midwifery background, let alone the fact that these were
her great-grandchildren. It is also worth noting, however,
that she was ninety years old at that time and that, together
with the very definite American/British culture differences, it
could appear unfair to judge her by this encounter.

It is clear, however, that Joan was not particularly warm
or loving, and all her grandchildren would say that any time
spent with her usually resulted in her giving them some coins
and sending them off to do something that did not include
her. Even Pamela had to call her mother by her first name.
It is unlikely these traits and the underlying unhappiness
that drove them would have occurred had Joan experienced
the childhood she was meant to. She should have been the
youngest of eight full siblings, the most loved of all, but from
two years old she lived in an orphanage, separated from any
natural love.

CHAPTER 23

Return to England

In 1960, Ben became unwell, and an eventual decision was made for Joan and Ben to go home to England, where they were likely to receive a health service they could afford. Ben had bladder cancer, thought to be related to torture he had endured as a prisoner of war. They sold up in Connecticut and, with their spaniel in tow, took the SS *Rotterdam* home to England in August, 1960. Sheila remembers seeing them off and being enthralled by the beauty and romance of the huge ship. She recognises that her love of cruising later in her life was the one benefit of her tepid relationship with her grandmother. At this time, the American family was not aware of the murders or that Joan had spent her first few years in an orphanage.

Joan and Ben settled in Malvern, Worcestershire, and bought 25 Queen's Road, a house with at least five bedrooms which they made into a care home for the elderly. Her mother, Florence, was, of course, her first lodger. The house was up the steep sides of Great Malvern and gave magnificent views across the Worcestershire countryside.

They had not been there long before Ben's illness took a turn for the worse, and in Ronkswood Hospital, Worcester, on the afternoon of 19th October, 1961, Ben died of renal failure and bladder cancer, aged fifty-three years. Ben, who had been a victim of his time, born in a land disputed and fought over and into a people who were to undergo their greatest challenge in history, who survived the rigours of capture and becoming stateless, was buried in Wilton Road Cemetery, Malvern, where a gravestone bearing his anglicised and Polish names remains, with a quote from the American engineer and poet, Rossiter Worthington Raymond.

'Marion Robert Benan née Zbigniew Zakrzewski. Life is eternal; and love is immortal; and death is only a horizon; and a horizon is nothing save the limit of our sight.'

At ninety, Florence may well have reflected on those words and how her horizon was getting closer, and how long ago it was when the horizon of six of her children vanished from her sight.

Being set on the side of the Great Malvern hill, the care home's position was not ideal for the elderly, with a challenging walk into town. However, Joan continued to run the establishment, which became a reasonably successful business. Her son, Peter, would make regular visits, largely when Joan needed some maintenance doing on the house. Peter's children would often accompany him and be frightened by the old ladies, particularly Florence, who, by then well in her nineties, had had an eye removed and wore no patch over the empty socket. To her young great-grandchildren who travelled often from Norfolk to visit, she was certainly a sight to remember.

On 14th March, 1970, Florence turned ninety-nine years old. With her remaining eye dimming, her own horizon closed in and, the day after her birthday, Florence Ellen Head died. Her great-grandchildren were disappointed she did not reach a hundred, but did not know the burden many of those ninety-nine years had carried.

Nearly sixty-five years
lost her children and hu
and whether she ever ha
is not known. Her fami¹
having a man friend in
went out for a drive ¡
during which there w
out of the vehicle. It ·
had decided not to b
a soul since her husl
had managed and thrived on n⌐
own industry. The catastrophic shock and traum⌐
experienced had given her strength and determination to
move only in her own direction and not ever be vulnerable
to such pain again. Florence was buried in the grounds of the
chapel in St Michael and All Angels, Martin Hussingtree. A
gravestone marks the spot and remembers her as '*One time
district nurse of this area*'.

In France, Monkey's husband, Lucien, had moved in with
his mistress and Monkey had moved out. The family say
Lucien initially moved his mistress into the garden chalet,
but the subsequent owners of Le Verger remember talk that
Monkey herself had had to live there. It seems more likely
that Lucien's lover was moved in first and then there was a
swap in the occupation of the garden chalet as the domestic
situation became intolerable for Monkey. She returned to
England and stayed in Malvern with Joan and her new man,
Ernest Moore.

Ernest (Ernie) Moore was forty-seven years old to Joan's
sixty-four when they married in Worcester Registry Office
on 3rd May, 1971. Their marriage certificate states he was a
chauffeur, but perhaps that was a term he used for driving the
hearses. He had been an ambulance driver, which is probably
how Joan met him. He was also homosexual.

Ernie had grown
recently lived in W
been killed in R
War while se
himself ser
Italy. H
if vis

up in Great Malvern, though he had
rcester. One of his brothers, Sidney, had
angoon, Burma, during the Second World
ving in the Gloucestershire Regiment. Ernie
ed as an orderly to an officer and saw service in
would often stay at ex-servicemen's establishments
ng London for various events.

as a gay man at that time, this marriage was convenient
Ernie and it provided Joan with a partner who supported
her in the business and eventually became her carer. Joan
did not like being alone and craved attention. The marriage
also helped Joan's dislike of being surrounded by people of
her own age. Whilst at that time Ernie was not open about
his homosexuality, Joan's family and those around him were
all aware. He was an accomplished baker and would have
been a significant help to Joan in the management of the care
home. Joan arranged for the nursing home to be signed over
to his name around the time of their marriage. Monkey was
aware of this and did not particularly approve. Monkey was
a witness at their marriage, as was Ernie's brother, William.
The marriage marked the last occasion on which Peter Robert
Head's name would be included on a British civil document,
some sixty-five years after his death.

Delicate at the best of times, the relationship between
Monkey and Joan deteriorated after the marriage. Monkey
took exception to Joan helping herself to her chic French
clothes and wearing them out and using some of her
belongings to decorate the home. Monkey retrieved her
items and, after giving some of the paintings she had brought
with her to her nephew, Peter, she packed and left for France.
France was her home, even with an estranged husband.

After selling Le Verger, her husband, Lucien, had bought
the house opposite, and it was there in 1978 that he was

found dead in a chair, bizarrely having been killed by a bolt of lightning that having bounced off the church, struck the house. Not having a will meant that all his estate, including the house, was passed to his sister and not to his wife, and Lucien's sister forbade Monkey from living in the house. Left with no option, she moved into a hotel in Vernon with few real possessions and only a little money.

Joan's health began to deteriorate in the late 1970s and Ernie took care of her till the end. She died in 1983, aged seventy-six years.

Joan had been born into a tumult, a lasting emotional chaos and vacuum, and for years she would have had no idea why. Most people, including her own children, never warmed to her, though they did make the effort to stay close. Her letters to her son Peter were lukewarm, yet they also felt as though they wanted to be warmer and more loving, but she just did not know how to do this. She had never learned how to. She had never been taught how.

> '... Perhaps you would like to come along Saturday or Sunday for a chat. I shall be in Saturday from 1.30 or if you come Sunday come in time for lunch usually 1.30 or 2pm. I only get meat every two weeks so can make sure that week of giving you a feed. Should you care to give me a ring any evening after 6 the number is 6304. Much love, affectionately Joan.'

She had been cast away herself by her mother as a two-year-old, yet at the opposite end of her mother's life she had kept her and cared for her to the end. She was very much a victim of something that happened before she was born. Joan had also experienced losing one of her own children in tragic accidental circumstances and suffered the rejection from her first husband and the death of her second. She had never learned how to express emotions to her children or grandchildren, though probably felt them anyway, but maybe could not understand them. Additionally, she lived in a time when mental health was not widely discussed. She had a need for partnership and quickly went from the loss of each husband to the next so as not to be alone.

Joan probably knew from an early age that the siblings she had not met were murdered brutally by her father, but had little understanding of it and only actually heard good things about her father. Almost certainly, Florence did not speak of it.

In her seventy-six years, she had been Frances Mary Head, Frances Joan Head, Frances Joan Cotterell, Frances Joan Zakrzewski, Frances Joan Benan and Frances Joan Moore. It is clear she was troubled and was looking for herself much of her life, with this search coming across as a sometimes selfish narcissistic behaviour. She had had little chance from the moment her father murdered her four brothers and two sisters, before she was born.

Joan's ashes were scattered in the churchyard of St Michael and All Angels, Martin Hussingtree, where her mother Florence lay.

The care home in Queen's Drive had been sold, and Joan and Ernie had bought a bungalow. A letter from Monkey suggests all Joan's real estate assets were put into Ernie's name at the time of their marriage. Ernie worked for the Spillsbury Funeral Company, where he was well respected and highly regarded. He always spoke well of Joan, almost in awe. His remaining days were spent in the company of a doctor with whom he lived until he died. In Ernie's will, his partner, Robert Smyth Pinches, inherited the house, and Joan's family never saw anything of the estate she had built up.

CHAPTER 24

Monkey's Final Days

Monkey would keep in contact with Peter by letter. Her letters were a mix of joy and disguised melancholy, but were very warm.

Passages such as, '*I wish you both a happy life with no bad periods*' could, in hindsight, be taken as reference to her own difficult past. She also always made reference to her name, signing off the letters, '*Lots of hugs and kisses, E Mathiot – P.S. Here in France (For years I have gone under the name of Monkey much to the disgust of the Queen Mother, now I am mostly called Madame, not at all funny)*.' The reference to 'Queen Mother' giving away the term she used for her own sometimes stern mother.

Monkey lived out her days in the hotel. With the hotel's daytime curfew policy, she would go for walks along the River Seine and into Vernon. Her mental capacity gradually began to decline, and while she would always come across as full of fun and to a certain degree sharp, her memory was beginning to fail.

Monkey had not spoken or written to Joan since leaving England. She replied to Peter, but did not post the letter immediately. In one of the two letters she had inadvertently written in reply to Peter's notification of Joan's death, she wrote a little about their relationship and how she felt that Joan had never really liked her. Her most poignant comment

131

was, 'Well I am the last one left now.' She did not comment further than that, but it seems likely that with the death of her younger sister, the death of all her other siblings became foremost in her mind. She had escaped on that day seventy-nine years earlier, and now, once again, had been left as the sole member of her generation.

'Dear Barbara and Peter

I have just received your letter, I can't believe it's possible, at least my sister's husband could have let me know she was undergoing operations, and that the outlook was serious. I suppose she will be buried in the same churchyard as mother up at Martin Fernhill Heath. Well I am the only one left now, and I will have to see out the days as best as I can. If I had a home it would not be so bad but as my husband died without making a will it was my sister in law who inherited, under French law and she sold the lot, so of course for me the only place left is the hotel. I go for long walks, the countryside is always so beautiful and I spend a lot of time walking along the banks of the river, I often see smart looking boats from England, unhappily it will soon be winter so I will have to return again to picture. There again there are some very good books at the library. If there are any mistakes in spelling please excuse I am forgetting my English. I will be able to remember the happy hours spent in your company and hope for the best of luck for you both and may the future be kind to you.

Yours very sincerely.

E Mathiot Monkey (That's the name I go by)'

Monkey died in January, 1989. What little she had left was bequeathed to Peter and Pamela. In another letter to Peter and Barbara after Joan's death, Monkey wrote, '*I hope my sister remembered she had a son and a daughter*', meaning that she hoped Joan's property had been left to her family. Joan had not, in an official capacity, remembered this. Monkey, however, did remember she had a niece and nephew. They were bequeathed a few photos of her home in Saint-Pierre-d'Autils, a ring, an out-of-place American Military Service Medal from the First World War (the story of which is lost in time) and a few remaining French Francs.

Elsa Mathiot was buried in the beautiful village cemetery in Saint-Pierre-d'Autils in the same grave as her husband, Lucien. This was also the grave of Dr Monier, for whom Monkey had worked for many years in Paris. Monkey's death marked the end of living memory of those associated with the events in Amesbury in 1905. At ninety-two, she had lived for eighty-four years after the incident that she had so fortunately avoided, and that incident had dictated how those eighty-four years would unfurl, starting with the unhappy time she spent in the orphanage. She never spoke to those dearest to her about the tragedy or about the abandonment, and she never judged her mother for it. She lived the only way she knew how, and that was to enjoy the now and survive all that was thrown at her.

Some years later, on 6th May, 2005, Peter and Barbara, together with Barbara's sister, Hilary, and her husband, Dennis, visited Amesbury cemetery. Peter had known a little about the murders for many years. Whatever it was he had been told when he was younger affected him so much that he had purposefully not told Barbara about it until long after their marriage, fearful she might reconsider marrying into a family that came from someone who could do such a thing.

If he had ever had any conversation with Monkey about the events, he had not told anyone. It is unlikely, and certainly in a phone call with Amy's grand-daughter, Liz, Peter said that Monkey had not spoken of the events.

He later learned more about the specifics and of Amy's existence around the centenary of the events and from contact with Jim Fuller.

It had taken a generation longer for Joan's descendants to reset themselves from the emotional trauma and turmoil that had started on that September evening before any of them were born, than it had for Amy, who had been alive at the time. Amy had spent years resetting herself, essentially living alone within other families, working hard as their cook. Then, when she was ready, she found, loved and gave a life of love and nurture. She had protected her two daughters from the knowledge as best as she felt right, thinking that to be the best course for them, protecting them with love. While at the end of her life her daughter Avis needed to know the secrets that her mother had hidden, she also knew that her own life had been happy.

Having grown up initially in an institution, Joan's emotional intelligence was different from the outset. She had not known how to write a better future for her children. Peter Cotterell and his sister, Pamela, had had to do that for themselves and, like Amy, had defied their upbringing by creating their own happy and loving families, and choosing to have a good life. Peter and Barbara had brought up four children, and Peter had enjoyed his motorcycles and cars and run a successful garage business in Norfolk.

Peter was in his eighties that day he stood by the grave. Supported by Barbara, his loving wife of so long, he placed some bright flowers on the grass by the stone inscribed with the name of his young uncles and aunts.

'Mildred Grace Head aged 10 years 8 months, Florence Ellen Head aged 7 years 9 months, William Robert Head 6 years 3 months, Peter Head aged 4 years 5 months, Alfred Head aged 2 years 9 months and Frederick George Head aged 9 months.'

Feet away from the remains of the six little Heads, with love around him and carrying the love of Monkey and the spirit of Florence and Joan within, Peter sobbed harder than his family had seen him do before. He cried for himself, for his unhappy childhood, for the six little Heads who did not have any chance of life, for the anguish of his mother, Monkey and Florence, and for his own brother Bobby, whom he had witnessed die so young. The sadness that had dwelled deep did not completely dissolve away in the tears he shed, but there was a catharsis and perhaps a line drawn in the sand.

Postscript

After the outpouring of grief and solidarity in Amesbury in September, 1905, the murders and suicide of Peter Head were quickly dropped from the memory of official records.

The town continued its rural life, and other murders and incidents replaced the Head tragedy as a topic of conversation. There was, for instance, in 1913, the nearby murder of Police Sergeant Crouch by PC Pike, who killed himself afterwards. Then the First World War arrived and changed everything. Boys of the lost Head sibling generation were slaughtered on an industrial scale, and that topic was the foremost conversation affecting every family in every village, town and city in Britain. The murder of the Head children slowly became lost in the collective memory of the town, only to resurface every other decade or so in a newspaper. When jesting, schoolchildren might sometimes mention the haunted field in South Mill Hill, but overall, the subject faded into history.

The six children had all been buried alongside their father in Amesbury Cemetery, but no stone was erected at the time to mark the spot, and therefore for many years there was no tangible reminder of the tragedy. The names of Mildred, Florence, William, Peter, Alfred and Frederick faded, and they became known collectively as the children murdered in the Amesbury tragedy.

I wonder if Charles Hallett later sometimes hesitated when returning children early to parents, or if Sergeant Scott took more opportunities to speak to people he saw changes in, or how many times the shock of finding the dead baby Frederick and his older sister, Florence, would visit PC Wells when he was on a night shift in some pitch-black lane or unlit street, or indeed in his restless sleep? I wonder if Dr Lockyer was that little bit more enquiring with some of his patients who he saw in stressful situations?

Would Peter Head have listened had Rev Fawkes been in the church when he visited and had been able to sit him down on that Friday and say to him, "Don't worry about your money, you are fine. In only a few years your elder children can work and help the family if it needs it. Do not end the lives and happiness of these children who love you so much and force a childhood in an orphanage for that little Monkey, who needs her freedom to excel, or for your unborn child who will always suffer from the lack of your presence. There are other ways. The muddle will pass and your family will flourish if you choose to allow them to live."

Would Peter Head have listened had Sergeant Scott taken him aside and asked him what ailed him and what had brought about the sudden sullenness he had noticed? Had Florence spoken to Dr Lockyer of the pains in the head Peter complained of, would he have held him back after an insurance man assessment and asked him about his head? Would it have changed the tide?

All these years later, we still read in the news about missed opportunities. On the outside, Peter was perfectly sane, and despite Sergeant Scott's astute observation, no one could have foreseen those tragic events. There is no doubt that intervention can sometimes help prevent mental health-related disasters. As a police hostage and crisis intervention negotiator, on many occasions I have stood on high buildings of various descriptions and spoken to people who are metaphorically and actually on the edge. Invariably, it takes several hours to earn the right to start influencing them that this is a permanent solution for a temporary problem and that there can be a life beyond their troubles. I once spoke to a man who was trying to cut his throat with a broken bottle, eventually persuading him to come with me to where mental health professionals could intervene. Two days later, he jumped in front of a train. It does not always work, but buying them time, providing intervention, is a lifeline that more often than not does succeed, whilst always remaining their choice.

From Peter's letters, it is clear that his concern was for himself and his perceived lack of opportunity and income. This we know was a vastly exaggerated pessimistic view of his condition. In his letters, he spoke of his suffering and of reverses. He spoke of domestic troubles in the same sentence as incorrectly commenting that his Prudential Insurance sales books were a mess. He didn't once speak of a fear or concern for the future of his children, and only spoke of his inability to be parted from them; certainly his sons anyway. The declared motive for his suicide was his outlook, perception of doom, fear for the future, dissatisfaction with life. His declared motive for murdering his children was simply a desire not to be parted from his sons. As if them all being dead kept them together. Physically, it actually did in the end, for they still all lie together.

Peter was a completely institutionalised man who clearly discovered that running every aspect of his own life was difficult. He had been raised by the church and then by the Army. When his business failed, he had become a beaten man, and this was just a little over one year after standing on a stage and receiving rapturous applause from an appreciative audience, and from all the men around him looking to him for guidance and instruction. He could not cope with all the decisions in real life and the consequences of those decisions. He could not cope with going from being a someone to, in his eyes, not being anyone.

There is evidence from Florence and (second-hand) from Stamp that Peter complained about pains in his head, and Peter spoke of losing his reason as a result of those pains. He never consulted a doctor. He didn't seek any kind of help. He continued until he did lose reason.

Florence spoke of Peter calling people who took their own lives 'cowards', and he himself signed off his letter to Stamp *'Yours (not a coward) P R Head'*. The label of a coward was significant to him and he went to lengths to not be so labelled, despite intending to do something where he had labelled others to be cowards. It is a sad and undeniable fact that people with mental anguish have a choice of doors through which they can travel to help relieve their pain, and one of those is the suicide route. There are arguments to be had as to whether or not the choice to use that door is a brave or cowardly decision; it is a highly complicated and probably subjective argument. Peter Robert Head, however, murdered six little children, having decided that he would kill himself, and because of a selfish desire not to be parted from at least four of them. The argument as to cowardice in this regard is perhaps less complicated.

After Jim Fuller wrote his account of the murders, his uncle, Rex Reynolds, a local builder, became very interested in the story. At one time, Rex had been a gravedigger and understood how they marked the burial sites with small stones under the grass, regardless of whether or not a memorial was erected. Jim and Rex studied the burial register for Amesbury Cemetery and compared the records and the grave numbers with the standing gravestones. They were able to identify the actual spot of the Heads' burial and then found a stone marker under the grass on which the correct reference number was engraved. Rex then paid for a gravestone to record the names of the children, and that gravestone stands today. Greatly affected by such an awful crime, Rex chose not to record Peter Robert Head's name on the stone, and it makes no mention of the murder. However, anyone passing and reading cannot fail to be intrigued by the same date of death being attached to six children. The stone erroneously records 22nd September as a Tuesday, when we know it was a Friday.

James William Henry Wells, that young Police Constable who searched for and made the grisly discovery of young Florence's body, completed his service in Wiltshire Police and retired to Water Works Road, Trowbridge, where he died in 1940. An obituary in a local newspaper mentioned that he had been the officer to find the bodies in Amesbury and that he had been so shocked he never spoke about the incident. His own family never knew about it until after his death.

Sergeant Walter Thomas Scott, the officer who recognised the madness rising in Peter Head, was promoted to Inspector of Bradford-on-Avon in 1907 and was a Superintendent by 1911. Throughout the First World War, Scott commanded the Warminster division of Wiltshire police. There he experienced a loss of staff to the armed services and more than a doubling in the population. The Magistrates' bench went from sitting monthly to daily. In 1918, he investigated the murder of a soldier by a colleague in Sutton Veny. The case was successfully prosecuted and the offender hanged. Scott received a commendation from the Director of Public Prosecutions as well as a £10 gratuity. He retired to Bournemouth in 1919 and, in a newspaper report about his lengthy career, the Head murders were mentioned. He died in Poole on 1st January, 1946, aged seventy-seven.

Superintendent Thomas Longstone was sixty years old when he helped to conduct the inquest. He retired in 1908 and lived in Devizes Road, Salisbury. He died on 14th May, 1921.

Charles William Hallett continued as headmaster until his retirement. He had been a good, thoughtful man and mentor. He died in 1933, aged seventy-seven, and was buried in Amesbury Cemetery with his wife and next to the subsequent burial of his son, who also taught in Amesbury School. Hallett's grave is within a few score metres of the Head children's burial place.

Doctor Gerard Edward Lockyer left Amesbury shortly after the murders and went on to practice at Much Wenlock, Shropshire. He retired in 1937 and lived with his sister and her husband, Annie and Robert Meikejohn. He died in a nursing home on 14th September, 1939, aged seventy.

Sergeant Major Henry Crossland Stamp served in India shortly after the murders and retired a few years later. He returned to his native Yorkshire and became a gamekeeper. After his wife died, he lived with his daughter in London, where he died in 1936.

Coroner Richard Arthur Wilson continued as coroner for some years and later followed in his father's footsteps again after he retired as coroner in 1910 by becoming Mayor of Salisbury. He continued running his substantial solicitor's firm in Salisbury. He died in the city in 1919.

Rev Fawkes left Amesbury for Poole very soon after the events of 1905. With the death of their own daughter in Amesbury that same year leaving a huge hole in their lives, he and his wife, Elizabeth, became very socially active in his new parish. He retired from being the vicar in 1910, though he undertook the occasional duty for the Diocese of Salisbury. In 1930, he was made Chairman of the Maternity and Child

Welfare Association in Poole. Mrs Fawkes was appointed the first female Magistrate in Poole in 1921, having been extremely generous with her time and energies to a number of associations. She was president of East Dorset National Council of Women Workers, as well as being active in the local branch of the NSPCC, the Dorset Mothers' Union, and the Girl Guides. Elizabeth died in 1932, aged eighty. Reginald Fawkes lived until 1939, when he died at the age of eighty-eight.

Algernon Charles Mainwaring Langton was the officiating vicar at the Heads' funeral. Afterwards, he became Rector of Langton, Lincolnshire, his ancestral home. He returned to Wiltshire in 1906 to marry the daughter of the vicar of Figheldean, near Salisbury. Rev Fawkes attended their wedding. Algernon remained in Langton until 1923, when he moved to become vicar of Mavis Enderby and Rathwaite from 1923 to 1946, when he retired to Shaftesbury, Dorset. He died there in 1948.

Edwin Henry James Read, the man from the Prudential who found Peter Head's books to be in order, died in 1928, aged seventy-three. Three of his four children had died before him, two in infancy. His son, George Lloyd Read, died the year before Edwin, aged forty-two. He had also been a superintendent for the Prudential.

Albert Edward King, Florence's brother, was very instrumental in the whole story. It was because he was living in Weymouth that Florence met Peter Head in the first place. Albert also had Peter's daughter, Amy, living with him at the time of the murders. He was no stranger to tragedy, having himself lost three of his seven children in infancy. He, of course, had the very grim task of identifying the bodies of the six little Head children and his brother-in-law, Peter. Albert died relatively young (in comparison with Florence) at fifty-six years old in 1922. One of his sons became a Sergeant Major in the Royal Artillery.

Barbara and Peter Cotterell raised their family in Norfolk. Barbara died in 2010. Before she died, Barbara wrote an account of her life for her children, an account that contributed so much to being able to describe the personalities of Monkey and Florence here. Peter died in 2021.

Peter Head's actions were truly awful and undefendable, and nearly one hundred and twenty years later the tail winds of the storm he started continue to blow, but even he, as a human, was more than that one day. All the people I have written about were so much more than what I have been able to convey from the traces of life that they, mostly inadvertently, left behind.

The exploration of those traces underlined to me the capability of human interaction; the importance of nurturing and dangers of selfishness; the power of love and kindness, and the malignance of indifference. It reinforced to me that it is often the most seemingly insignificant interactions in life that can have the most lasting positive effects. They are just rarely measured and recorded, and often are lost in the mayhem of history.

Acknowledgements

The first acknowledgement must go to the unknown journalist of one of the Salisbury newspapers who wrote the singularly comprehensive report of the inquest hearing. The inquest file itself has long been destroyed and, as such, without the work of this journalist who transcribed the hearing and the letters Peter left behind for the newspaper, we would have very little knowledge about what happened on 22nd September, 1905.

I am very grateful to all Peter Robert Head's descendants who have helped me on this journey, who patiently acknowledged and answered my continuous emails and provided their memories; and, more so, for their blessing for me to pursue this project: Liz Mathias and Gill Davies, grandchildren of Amy Edith Flavell, and for the photographs of her; Wendy Hayden and Grant Cotterell, children of Peter Cotterell, for their photographs, letters from Monkey and the wonderful diaries of their mother, Barbara, as well as also putting up with my endless emails and random thoughts; Sheila Ahearn, Pamela's daughter and grand-daughter of Joan and William Cotterell, for her American memories of Florence and Joan.

To Jim Fuller, who wrote the first booklet about the murders, for keeping the story in the public eye as much as he could and finding the location of the graves with his late uncle, Rex Reynolds, and also for the many, many emails we shared and his enthusiasm for re-examining the incident and my filling in the gaps. His extensive knowledge of Amesbury and its history, together with his kind enthusiasm for my research, has been essential in the production of this book. Jim's interest in local history had been influenced by his grandfather, Thomas Lionel Fuller, who was an early photographer of the area. Postcard photographs that T.L. Fuller took are still a great primary source of visual history of the area. He had come to Amesbury in 1911 and married Jim's grandmother, Harriett Wallen, who was very much a native of the town. Harriett, born in 1895, attended Amesbury School and would have known the Head children, being the same age as Mildred Grace Head. She was most probably in her class. The story of the murders had filtered down to Jim's father, also Thomas Lionel Fuller, who would sometimes mention it to Jim when driving past the track in South Mill Hill Road. I found a copy of Jim's book in the Swindon and Wiltshire History Centre in Chippenham and read it with great interest. Jim's address was on his book, and so I cold-called him. I visited the very day he was moving house, so was lucky to have found him to speak with.

The staff of the fantastic Swindon and Wiltshire History Centre in Chippenham, often getting out material I needed to look at, at late notice. Always extremely cordial and helpful. The library is the most wonderful resource centre for local history.

To Robin Dunn, who lives in Le Verger, Saint-Pierre-d'Autils, for kindly inviting me in when I cold-called there in 2022, and for showing me around the house and gardens where Monkey lived.

I thank Isabelle O'Sullivan for translating the French documents I acquired in the research.

I am grateful to Sister Mary Joy, the current incumbent of the Sisters of Bethany, who provided me with some of the history of the institution and confirmed the dates of Monkey's and Joan's time there.

To John Porter, archivist for Prudential, who provided me with some historic context of the company, and also trawled their records for reference to Peter Head.

To Barbara Jauncy of St Michael and All Angels, Martin Hussingtree, for helping me locate Florence Head's grave. The first time I visited Florence's grave, the headstone was standing up and could be read. I revisited a year later having written most of this text, and found her headstone had fallen face down and cannot be read at the moment. I hope this was not a message of disapproval from Florence for writing this.

I am grateful to Cathi Poole and Clare Brayshaw of York Publishing for their excellent communications, and assistance in the process, and to editor Claire Waring, and proof reader Phil Clinker who edited my myriad typos, spelling and grammatical errors with such efficiency.

To my friend Ellie Lawrenson, whose genealogy led me to this story whilst I researched her great-great-grandfather, Frances Everett.

I'd like to thank the fantastic authors Jon Stock and Lucinda Hawksley for affording me time to chat, thereby providing me with heaps of inspiration and enthusiasm.

Also to those good friends and family who read my various versions of manuscript and offered feedback. In particular to Dee Meaden for her considerable help and mentorship.

Finally, to my long-suffering wife, Ann, who has endured four years of me talking about Peter Head and asking her why she thought he did it. For her encouragement, support and love.

Neil Berrett
Wiltshire, 2024

Bibliography

Fuller, James. *The South Mill Hill Murders: A Tragedy at Amesbury*. Self-published.

Chandler, John and Goodhugh, Peter (1979). *Amesbury: History and Description of a South Wiltshire Town*. The Amesbury Society.

Leachman, E.W. (1915). *St. Peter's Bournemouth*. Sydenham.

McQueen, Ian (1971). *Bournemouth St Peter's*. Dorset Publishing Company.

Peitzman, Steven J. (1989). 'From dropsy to Bright's disease to end-stage renal disease'. *Milbank Quarterly*, Vol 67, Suppl 1, pp 16-32. (https://pubmed.ncbi.nlm.nih.gov/2682170/).

Jones, Margaret C. (2022). *The Adventurous Life of Amelia B. Edwards, Egyptologist, Novelist, Activist*. Bloomsbury.

https://www.britishbattles.com/war-in-egypt-and-sudan/battle-of-tel-el-kebir/

https://www.workhouses.org.uk/StMarylebone/

About the author

Neil Berrett served for over thirty years as a police officer in the Wiltshire Police. He now works as an actor and writer. A lifelong genealogist, he still actively researches his own and others' family trees.